T·H·E·O·F·F·I·C·I·A·L

COUCH POTATO COOKBOOK

BY

Mary Beth Jung,
Melinda Corey,
and Jackie Ogburn

Illustrated by
Robert Armstrong

Foreword by Jack Mingo

PROLONGED VIEWING

Couch POTATOES ®

SIC SEMPER POTATVM RECLINVS

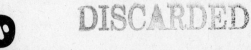

WARNER BOOKS
A Warner Communications Company

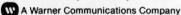

A Blue Cliff Editions book.

Copyright © 1988 Blue Cliff Editions, Inc.

Couch Potato and Couch Potatoes are registered trademarks of Robert Armstrong. All rights reserved. Used under authorization.

Book design by Nina Clayton.

The COCOPUFS Report has no relation to the breakfast cereal.

Warner Books, Inc.,
666 Fifth Avenue, New York, NY 10103

A Warner Communications Company

Printed in the United States of America
First printing: October 1988
10 9 8 7 6 5 4 3 2 1

Library of Congress Cataloging in Publication Data
Jung, Mary Beth.
The official Couch Potato cookbook/Mary Beth Jung, Melinda Corey, and Jackie Ogburn; illustrated by Robert Armstrong; foreword by Jack Mingo.
p. cm.
On t.p. the registered trademark symbol "TM" is superscript following "Potato" in the title.
"Blue Cliff Editions book."
ISBN 0-446-38927-7
1. Quick and easy cookery. 2. Snack foods. I. Corey, Melinda.
II. Ogburn, Jackie. III. Title.
TX652.J857 1988   88-14710
641.5′55—dc19   CIP

Contents

Acknowledgments

There are many friends who helped to make this book possible.

First, we want to thank Jason Shulman, who supported this project from its conception. This book would not have been possible without his perseverance.

Liv Blumer, our editor, and Kate Wheble, her assistant, provided invaluable enthusiasm and editorial suggestions.

We thank our COCOPUFS researchers for their exactitude and intestinal fortitude.

Our friends who contributed to the "Foods for Watching Alone" section deserve a special thanks, both for admitting that they eat these strange concoctions and for offering us recipes for them: Susan Carton, Melanie Smith, Rick Starr, and Jon Winser.

Finally, we express our gratitude to our husbands, Lou Ganser, George Ochoa, and Ben Deahl, for editing our copy, contributing passages, and tasting our recipe creations.

—M.B.J., M.C., and J.O.

A VIEW FROM THE COUCH

by Jack Mingo

Minister of Information and
Propaganda of the Couch Potatoes

As one of the world's foremost authorities on the Couch Potato movement, having written two books and dozens of articles on the subject, I am often asked about the origins of the concept and phrase.

Actually, I'm lying. Rarely am I asked about it. And usually only by some early-morning radio DJ who has awakened me for a quick on-air interview at some ungodly hour when there's nothing to watch on TV but snow, evangelists, and test patterns. Since I am only marginally coherent even at my peak hours (during prime-time commercial breaks mostly), I never answer particularly well. Which is annoying, because I love to tell the story.

Most people assume that "Couch Potato" sprang mysteriously from the air. They seem surprised to hear that real people like themselves invented it, nurtured it, and brought it to international attention without corporate sponsorship, a multimillion-dollar PR budget, or anything more than a good idea and the willingness to spread the word.

"Couch Potato" was coined spontaneously during the early 1970s by Bob Armstrong and a small group of buddies in Pasadena, California. They would get together to watch TV long into the night and into the next day. One good-naturedly insulted another, little knowing that the epithet would eventually become a moniker millions would wear proudly.

The term remained a private joke for a few years before beginning to leak slowly into the culture. In 1976 an organization called "The Couch Potatoes" was formed by Bob Armstrong and Al Dodge and the group of buddies became the nine Couch Potato Elders, serving for life. Membership grew slowly, fed by references in the underground comics of Bob Armstrong. In 1979 the group was represented in Pasadena's Doo-Dah Parade, the local counterculture's answer to the Rose Bowl Parade. The Spuds later dropped out when parade officials ruled out both motorized floats and generators for the TV sets.

In 1980, the Couch Potato leadership decided the conditions were ripe for emerging from our underground viewing rooms and taking our lifestyle to the public. The time seemed right: Freddy Silverman's vision of good TV ruled the airwaves and a man who once had his own TV show was the President. We felt we should lie down and be counted. As far as we were concerned, the recline of Western Civilization had begun.

At that time, we wanted to put out a video communiqué, figuring that would be the best way to reach our natural allies, but that ended up being impractical. Instead, in 1982, we settled on a newsletter for our members and supporters, with each article short enough to be read during a commercial break.

It was successful beyond its small circulation. Beth Ann Krier of the *Los Angeles Times* read it and wrote a feature article that was syndicated nationally and overseas. The rest of the media jumped aboard, including such disparate journals as the *London Times*, *TV Guide*, and the *National Enquirer*. For a while we seemed to spend more time appearing on TV than watching it, with spots on "The Tonight Show," "PM Magazine," "Entertainment Tonight," and a host of other shows.

I wrote a book, *The Official Couch Potato™ Handbook,* to explain and celebrate those of us who find the people on TV more fascinating than our own friends and families. Published in 1983 by a small publisher in Santa Barbara, it led to a second book, *The Couch Potato™ Guide to Life.*

The next logical step in the Couch Potato publishing program was this book, *The Official Couch Potato™ Cookbook.* It is chock-full of good eating ideas, with recipes especially tailored for crucial shows in any good Couch Potato's viewing regimen. These recipes can be prepared before prime time, during station breaks, season openers, and pledge breaks—times when we traditionally do whatever needs to be done to keep health and hearth intact.

The Couch Potato membership have long given deep thought to set-side eating. Over the years, we have paid respect to pioneers of video vittles— people such as Clarence Birdseye, a pioneer of frozen food, George Munsey, who invented the toaster oven, and Gilbert Swanson, the man who developed and named the TV dinner. Not to mention the Couch Potatoes' own food guru, Chef Aldo, who was the first to postulate that a typical Tuber can eat his or her own weight in less than a week of prolonged video viewing.

These recipes are well within this proud tradition, yet they are new and different, developed for the discriminating Potato. While they embody the convenience and ease of preparation that championship TV viewers demand, these recipes are classy enough to serve to your family, friends, or even that special guest who's coming over to watch *8½* on your 26-inch Zenith.

So purchase this book, take it home, and feast your mouth the next time you're feasting your eyes. It might be the best buying decision you've made since you treated yourself to that satellite dish, that widescreen TV, and that lifetime subscription to *TV Guide.*

INTRODUCTION

Couch Potatoes are more fortunate than most humans. They have found their reasons for living—to watch TV and to eat. Their only problem is: what to eat?

In pre-Couch Potato days, mobility was a virtue, so people traveled to their meals. During the week, they noshed at the local McDonald's, Taco Bell, and Pizza Hut; on the weekend, they made reservations at swanky restaurants or enjoyed international foods at the mall. The positive effect of this era was that people learned more about tastes and cuisines; the negative effect was that traveling to restaurants left them exhausted. They spent so much time exercising their palates and finding parking spaces that there was no time for the more important things in life, like watching TV.

Fortunately, the Couch Potato Age has changed all that. Inertia has replaced mobility; the sofa has dethroned the fast-food stop; and staying in has triumphed over going out. But in the midst of this revolution, whither cuisine? Without the franchise and the world-class restaurant, there is only . . . *the kitchen*.

Some of you remember the kitchen, that wonderful place where warm, satisfying meals came from when you were a child. Now that you've been trained to dine out instead of eat in, the kitchen is an alien land. Its treasures are tantalizing but elusive. Tubers love good food. But preparing it takes time, and that's one thing you don't have. You need to devote your energies to sustained TV viewing. A simple casserole from *The 60-Minute Gourmet* means missing all of "Cheers" and half of "L.A. Law."

What busy Couch Potatoes need is a way to unite their two loves—TV watching and good food—with a cuisine that answers both their lifestyle needs.

That's exactly why *The Official Couch Potato™ Cookbook* was born. It offers the only cuisine developed for the busy TV watcher who is also a serious, sophisticated eater.

A Dish for Every Time Slot

Just as man cannot live by bread alone, so the Couch Potato gourmet cannot live by snacks alone. The appeal of even Ruffles with Green Onion Dip would dim if it were served at every meal. That is why we have searched the globe for the finest international and regional American specialties and carefully adapted them for easy preparation during the major breaks in daily television programming.

An average evening of television dining might begin with some "Station Break Sprints," simple snacks that can be prepared easily during the 360 seconds of commercials that punctuate the hour- and half-hour-long shows. For light situation comedies, such as "The Cosby Show," we feature O Sole Theo Pizza, while for cop shows, we offer Mirandized Spiced Nuts, a tempting concoction of peanuts tossed with tangy spices inspired by law-and-order's most controversial ruling.

Later in the evening, when you're in that 30-minute video void known as "Waiting for 'L.A. Law,'" we put you in a West Coast mood with some fresh and simple California-style specialties, such as a Closed Case Sandwich, a side dish of L.A. Slaw, or our fruity and aromatic Valencia Orange Shortbread.

To settle into "Late-Night Viewing," you can skip an uninteresting feature on the 11 o'clock news to prepare a soothing comfort drink such as Koppel Cocoa or Letterman's Spiked Cider. The "Reruns" snacks that round out the early morning hours are just as calming: they've been carefully designed to match the TV classic for which they're named. The Trekkie Trail Mix, with its blend of dried apples, banana chips, and peanuts can sustain you as you boldly go where no man has gone before, while the Odd Couple Heroes inspire thoughts of a New York deli run by Oscar and Felix themselves. And, true to their origins, the Honeymooners' Munch Mix and Beaver Cleaver's Brownie à la Mode come only in black and white.

Some television shows are so important that they can only be properly viewed by a group. Playoffs, season openers, and the next new episode of

"Moonlighting" are all events worthy of group celebration. For these events, we have created "The Couch Potato Party Planner," with menus tailored specifically to each event. For example, the "Super Bowl Party" features a constant stream of hearty food, all of which can be prepared during the many boring breaks in the game. The frequent two minute time-outs that used to annoy are now the time to prepare the Two Minute Time-Out Dip and the plodding half-time marching band affords time to prepare the Super Sloppy Joes and Macho Nachos. "The *It's a Wonderful Life* Party" menu, on the other hand, features happy, soothing food that celebrates Christmas and guardian angels, such as Clarence's Flaming Rum Punch and the deliciously light Guardian Angel Cookies.

Some of the recipes in *The Official Couch Potato™ Cookbook* use the microwave oven and the food processor, two very Couch Potato-friendly inventions. But we realize that not every household has these high-tech Tuber appliances, and most of the recipes in this book don't call for them. For those that specify microwave, we have provided the conventional oven cooking times and temperatures as well. For those that suggest a food processor, knives are the alternate choice.

Matching good recipes with programming breaks and types of shows, this book unites food and culture in a new cuisine: Couch Potato Food.

Safe Eating

Culinary and aesthetic triumphs are only part of Couch Potato cooking. There is, finally, a more serious side to this new cuisine, which has to do with the health and safety of Tubers as they eat.

A recent study by the Council of Couch Potatoes United for Food Safety (COCOPUFS) surveyed the habits of Couch Potato eating and revealed the following:

1. They eat in large quantities.
2. They frequently injure themselves and their property on poorly designed food.

We have used these COCOPUFS findings as guidelines for developing and testing Couch Potato foods for this book. No recipe was awarded the Official Couch Potato Seal of Approval until it met the following criteria:

1. *The food can be prepared in large quantities.* We applaud the healthy attitude that Couch Potatoes have toward eating. They are loyal to the foods they like and eat them in copious amounts. That is why we have designed most of the recipes to yield four to six servings. This, we believe, will be an adequate amount for one or two Tubers at a sitting. For families or Couch Potato parties, recipes can be easily doubled, tripled, or increased exponentially.

2. *The food requires little hand-to-eye coordination to eat.* As the COCOPUFS study indicated, the major safety problem with poorly designed food is its high injury level to furniture, clothes, and especially the mouth. That is why we have eliminated all foods that can leak, scratch, or jab the eater. Each Couch Potato food has been scientifically scaled to glide easily down the throat, not onto the sofa or carpet. For example, the Marple Mushroom Broil is prepared on an English muffin, with safe, rounded edges, so it won't injure the sides of the mouth. The Mystery Chip Cookies are designed to fit into the mouth whole, so there are no crumbs. Even "The Wide World of Sports Parties" foods are soft enough so that they don't chip the teeth when chomped in anger or damage the screen when flung after a referee's bad call.

As a service to Couch Potatoes, we have included excerpts from "The COCOPUFS Report," a scientific survey of 25 favorite snack foods, rated according to health and safety criteria.

Ever since Ralph Kramden sat in front of his new television set and surrounded himself with snacks, food has been the natural accompaniment to television. The vicissitudes of the past 30 years—outdoor barbecues, health food crazes, and nouvelle cuisine—temporarily sidetracked television cookery. Couch Potato culture has brought us back to basics. Not only has it restored food to the easy chair, where it belongs, but it has added the variety and quality that food lovers deserve.

Welcome to Couch Potato food, the cuisine of the new and improved television-watching generation.

PRIME TIME

Prime-Time—that magical span when, released from the grind of nine-to-five, you plant yourself, as do millions of other Americans, in front of the television and drink in the offerings of the major networks. These are the witching hours when ordinary bankers and nurses, teachers and truck drivers, shed their workaday identities and become Couch Potatoes, swept into worlds of glamour and fantasy, comedy and drama, news and weather, action and suspense. But wait . . . what's wrong with this picture?

Something is missing. A commercial break comes and suddenly it hits you—you have nothing to eat! The show has started again and you can't miss this next crucial scene. What to fix? What food could possibly be compatible with the exquisite lassitude of TV-watching? Never fear, *The Official Couch Potato™ Cookbook* will help you out of these dire straits.

The heady hours of early evening leave little time for puttering in the kitchen, a condition that inspired us to create the "Station Break Sprints," quick and filling food that can be made during commercial breaks. For those who know that Trivial Pursuit® will never be in the same league as "Jeopardy," we have a selection of "Million-Dollar Game Show Snacks." To suit the tonier tastes of PBS watchers, we offer "Pledge-Drive Specials," treats that take a little longer to prepare, neatly removing you from the couch during the tedious pledge-drive pitches.

Finally, recognizing that sometimes even prime time fails you, scheduling something dreadful in the time slot before your favorite series, we give you "Waiting for 'L.A. Law.'" Take advantage of this down time by preparing some of these treats in anticipation of the pleasure that awaits you when the boring program is over.

Armed with this book, you need never suffer another evening of less than the best that Couch Potato life has to offer.

STATION BREAK SPRINTS

When you are struck with hunger pangs in the middle of your favorite show, don't despair or (Heaven forbid!) go hungry—simply concoct one of our delicious "Station Break Sprints." These hearty, mouth-watering recipes are designed to be prepared, from raw ingredients to snack-tray service, within six minutes which is precisely the time from the closing credits of your average sitcom to the opening scene of your basic crime show (30-second pause for an Isuzu commercial included).

We've created a wide variety of "Station Break Sprints," from toothsome main courses such as O Sole Theo Pizza and the Gordon Shumway Sandwich to lighter but no less fulfilling snacks such as Miss DiPesto's Guacamole and Cajun Popcorn. The straightforward J.B. Fletcher calls for an equally reliable snack such as the smooth and fruity "Ice Cream," She Wrote, while hot and trendy detective shows such as "Miami Vice" require the cooling taste of our Miami Ice.

All of these foods, no matter what the cuisine or food type, aspire to TV watchers' highest ideal: to eat *and* watch simultaneously, even when faced with the most severe time constraints. "Station Break Sprints" do that, and more: they satisfy your fondest spudly food desires.

Miss DiPesto's Guacamole

(Miss DiPesto's Pesto would have been too obvious.)

If you find you're hurried
'Cause you're really worried
That you'll miss the baddie
Threaten David and Maddie
While you're up from your seat
Concocting a treat,
There's no need to fear,
Miss DiPesto is here.
"Take a big avocado"—
That's this recipe's motto—
Tomato and lemon,
And you'll think you're in heaven.
You'll say, "Holy moly,"
Eating this guacamole.
Well, I've got to run now,
The station break's done now.

Preparation time: 5 minutes

2 ripe avocados, chilled
2 tbs lemon juice
1 small ripe tomato, seeded and chopped
1 clove garlic, chopped
Salt to taste
Medium to hot salsa

1 Halve avocados lengthwise. Remove pit and scoop meat from shell.

2 In a small bowl, mash avocados and lemon juice with a fork. There should be a few lumps remaining.

3 Stir in remaining ingredients. If desired, add 1 to 2 tablespoons salsa to add spice to the dip. Cover with plastic wrap and chill until ready to serve with tortilla chips.

Yield: 4 servings

Mirandized Spiced Nuts

These spicy peanuts with their unrelenting crunch were created to honor that satisfying moment in all good cop shows when one of the partners looks the unrepentant scumbag in the face and growls, "Read 'im his Mirandas."

Preparation time: 6 minutes

1 egg white, slightly beaten
1 tsp water
¾ cup sugar
1 tsp cinnamon
1 tsp ginger
½ tsp nutmeg
½ tsp allspice
1½ cups salted, roasted peanuts

1 Combine all ingredients in a large skillet or frying pan.

2 Heat mixture over medium heat, stirring constantly, until the nuts are coated and the mixture is dry.

3 Remove to a cookie sheet to cool. Break nuts apart if necessary. Do not cool on paper towels as nuts will stick to towels.

Yield: 2 cups

O Sole Theo Pizza

Theo Huxtable is better known for getting into scrapes while showing off for the girls than for his ability in the kitchen. This pizza is so quick and easy that even the most impatient, starving teenage boy can whip it up and impress his friends with his cooking.

Preparation time: microwave oven—6 minutes
conventional oven—10 minutes

½ pita bread, split horizontally
2 tbs minced onion
2 tbs diced green pepper
1 small clove garlic, minced
1 tsp olive oil
1 small plum tomato, diced
¼ tsp dried basil or 1 tsp finely minced fresh basil
3 tbs smoked mozzarella cheese, shredded

1 Toast the split pita pieces under broiler. Set aside.

2 Combine onion, green pepper, garlic, and oil in microwave dish. Microwave on high for 2 minutes. Add tomatoes and basil and microwave for 1 minute more. For conventional oven, sauté onion, green pepper, and garlic in oil for 3 minutes, then add tomato and basil and sauté 1 minute more.

3 Place pita on a microwave plate or paper towel. Spread vegetable mixture on pita and top with cheese. Microwave until cheese melts, about 30 seconds. For conventional oven, place pita on a broiler pan and top with vegetable mixture and cheese. Broil 4 inches from heat for 2 to 3 minutes.

Yield: 1 serving

Gordon Shumway™ Sandwich

When there was a shortage of cats on Melmac, ALF™ would prepare this high-tech variation of that old standby, the BLT. The Gordon Shumway is easier to eat because there's no slippery lettuce to cause the bacon to fall out. Make sure you position the cheese so it melts over the bacon and tomato and bonds everything together.

**Preparation time: microwave oven—3 minutes
conventional oven—15 minutes**

2 slices bacon
1 slice whole-wheat bread, toasted
1 small tomato, sliced
2 ozs sharp cheddar cheese, sliced

1 Cook bacon in microwave or in a frying pan on the stove, according to package directions.

2 Place tomatoes, bacon, and cheese on toasted bread.

3 Microwave on high until cheese melts, about 20 to 30 seconds. For conventional oven, place cheese, tomatoes, and bacon on toasted pita and broil 4 inches from the heat for 3 to 4 minutes.

Yield: 1 sandwich

Miami Ice

It's Friday night, fantasy time, and you're ready for another episode of "Miami Vice," with cool cops, hot crooks, and tropical designer colors. This frosty drink whips up into a smooth pink as cool as Sonny Crockett's pastel shirts.

Preparation time: 2 minutes

1 10-oz package frozen strawberries in syrup, still frozen but cut into chunks
1 medium ripe banana

1 cup milk
1 cup plain yogurt

1 Place all ingredients into a blender container. Cover and blend at the highest speed until smooth.
2 Serve immediately in a tall glass filled with crushed ice.
Yield: 4 servings

Turtle Tarts

"Moonlighting" is one of our favorite shows, but when an episode *without* Maddie or David is aired for the third time in one year, these Turtle Tarts are needed. The caramel provides the solace that one of their old-fashioned arguments used to bring and the crème de cacao offers an adequate substitute for the missing plot.

Preparation time: microwave oven—6 minutes
conventional stove—10 minutes

½ lb individually wrapped caramels
½ cup light cream
2 tbs crème de cacao
1½ cups toasted pecans, finely chopped
6 ready-to-serve 3-inch tart shells
Whipped cream

1 Unwrap caramels and combine with cream in a microwave-safe dish. Microwave on high until smooth, about 3 to 4 minutes. On stove top, melt caramels and cream over low heat in a double boiler, stirring constantly.
2 Stir in crème de cacao and nuts. Pour into shells.
3 Cool. Serve with whipped cream, if desired.
Yield: 6 servings

"Ice Cream," She Wrote

They all scream for this one—a light and fruity cross between grainy Italian gelato and smooth, comforting Carvel ice cream. Try it when "Murder She Wrote" travels to Italy.

Preparation time: 1 minute

> *6 ozs frozen, unsweetened strawberries or*
> *sliced peaches, unthawed*
> *¼ cup heavy cream*
> *2 tbs confectioners' sugar*

1 Place all ingredients in a food processor.
2 Cover and blend until smooth, about 30 seconds. Serve immediately.

Yield: 2 servings

Ode to Popcorn

Popcorn holds an honored place in the Couch Potato diet. It meets these three primary criteria: it can be fixed quickly, consumed in large quantities, and requires little hand-eye coordination to eat. Popcorn can be popped in a variety of ways. There is a method to suit every type of Couch Potato from the traditionalist with hot oil and a large pot, to the purist with a hot-air popper, to the high-tech Tuber with a microwave. Quick and easy to fix, just a few minutes' effort produces a huge bowl of crunchy white corn. Popcorn is nearly the perfect Couch Potato food.

Popcorn has only one significant drawback. Eaten in its pure state, freshly popped and unadorned, popcorn is boring. There are those who defend it, saying that it still delivers crunch and fulfillment in its pristine form. (These are obviously the same people who believe that tofu is a legitimate foodstuff and that lima beans are fit for human consumption.)

Those of us who know better realize that exciting popcorn depends on toppings and that the foundation of all good toppings is butter.

Butter is what enables the toppings to cling to popcorn, be it a classically simple sprinkle of salt or an exotic Chinese five-spice topping. New, so-called "improved" methods of popping, especially with hot-air machines, make butter more necessary than ever. The traditional hot oil method left a thin coating of oil on most kernels, enough for salt to cling without other assistance. New no-oil popping methods leave the puffs virtually topping-repellent. By themselves, most toppings glide off and rest at the bottom of the bowl, uneaten and unenjoyed. Butter is the necessary bonding agent that brings the crunch and the flavor together.

We give you these new toppings, all with liberal amounts of butter, to save you from boring popcorn. In popcorn as in life, variety is the spice.

Italian Popcorn

Popular rumor to the contrary, undercover wiseguy Vince Terranova did not have to eat this popcorn five times a day as part of his initiation into the Mob.

Preparation time: 6 minutes

> ⅓ cup unpopped popcorn
> 1½ tbs butter
> ¼ tsp onion powder
> ¼ tsp garlic powder
> 2 tbs grated Parmesan cheese

1 Pop popcorn according to your favorite method. Set aside in serving bowl.

2 Melt butter in a small frying pan.

3 Add onion and garlic powders to butter and stir until well mixed. Be careful not to let the butter burn.

4 Pour butter mixture over popcorn and toss. Sprinkle Parmesan cheese over popcorn and toss again. Serve immediately.

Yield: 6½ cups

Dragon Breath Popcorn

When you are watching yet another Oriental mini-series, like "Shogun" or "Noble House," try this meeting of East and West, American popcorn and Chinese spices. Five-spice powder is a mix of star anise, cinnamon, cloves, fennel, and peppercorns, available at gourmet shops. Blended with butter, it makes a tangy topping for popcorn.

Preparation time: 6 minutes

> *⅓ cup unpopped popcorn*
> *1½ tbs butter*
> *½ tsp Chinese five-spice powder*

1 Pop popcorn according to your favorite method. Set aside in serving bowl.

2 In a small frying pan, melt butter.

3 Add Chinese five-spice powder to butter and stir until well mixed. Be careful not to let the butter burn.

4 Pour butter mixture over popcorn, and toss. Serve immediately.

Yield: 6½ cups

Cajun Popcorn

This popcorn is sneaky. It doesn't seem that hot when you first crunch it, but it has a wicked afterburn. You may have to excuse yourself to fetch another glass of iced tea to cool your throat.

Preparation time: 6 minutes

> *⅓ cup unpopped popcorn*
> *1½ tbs butter*
> *¼ tsp Tabasco® sauce*
> *¼ tsp cayenne pepper*
> *¼ tsp garlic powder*

1 Pop popcorn according to your favorite method. Set aside in serving bowl.
2 In a small frying pan, melt butter.
3 Add Tabasco® sauce, cayenne pepper, and garlic powder to butter and stir until well mixed. Be careful not to let the butter burn.
4 Pour butter mixture over popcorn, toss thoroughly, and serve immediately.

Yield: 6½ cups

Million-Dollar Game Show Snacks

After a rough day in the real world (which can include everything from battling bumper-to-bumper afternoon traffic to watching Oprah Winfrey), a Couch Potato needs to ease into the evening. There's no better way than vicariously winning several thousand dollars on an evening game show.

Game shows are the ultimate Couch Potato relaxer. They are comfortably familiar: watching "Wheel of Fortune" or "The New Newlywed Game" five evenings a week is like a regular after-dinner chat with an old friend. Game shows also know how to take your mind off your troubles. It is difficult to worry about regrouting the bathroom floor when you are trying to come up with the question for "He was the only President to use Grecian Formula 16." They also let you be a winner. When your sales projections are off by 500 percent and your child has just entered the food-throwing stage, you can at least triumph in the knowledge that you have beaten the nuclear physicist, aspiring actress, and medical librarian tonight on "Jeopardy."

Such tireless friends of the world-weary Tuber can be properly honored only with snacks that offer as much satisfaction and reward as they do. That is our guiding principle behind these Million-Dollar Game Show Snacks. We bring together the flavors and textures that early evening Tubers love most—sweet, salty, crunchy, and smooth—in three snacks that will complement your favorite evening game shows. Our light and sugary Vanna's White Wheels will coordinate with whatever Vanna wears that night. The Hollywood Cheese Squares are just as tangy as any of Joan Rivers's (or the late Paul Lynde's) retorts. To top everything off, we offer the Don Pardo Cooler, a smooth lemon and lime concoction that was created to honor the famous announcer of the original "Jeopardy," probably the only man to make a fortune by uttering the words, "Back to you, Art."

Just as each week's roster of game shows is taped during one day of shooting, so these Million-Dollar Game Show Snacks are easy to make ahead of time. Each recipe can be prepared during an uninteresting hour block of programming and then savored throughout the week. With these treats, you no longer will have to settle for the 100 cans of Spam that lie behind Cupboard Number Three.

Hollywood Cheese Squares

Old game shows never die, they just resurface with a new host and more neon. The new "Hollywood Squares" is really just a version of "To Tell the Truth" with a three-story set. Our Hollywood Cheese Squares are an updated combination of favorite cheeses spread in a circle on a crisp cracker square.
Preparation time: 4 minutes

1 8-oz package cream cheese, softened
1 4-oz package blue cheese
1 cup sharp Cheddar cheese, shredded
2 tbs sherry wine
1 tsp Worcestershire sauce
1 clove garlic, minced
Dash onion powder

1 In a mixing bowl or food processor, blend all ingredients until light and fluffy.
2 Chill or serve immediately on salted wheat crackers.
Yield: 10 servings

Don Pardo Cooler

This cool citrus drink salutes the smoothest announcer in television game shows and the only man who ever knew all the correct questions for "Jeopardy" answers. Members of the Don Pardo Fan Club sip it every night during the new version of "Jeopardy" to keep the Pardo spirit alive.

Preparation time: 3 minutes

1 6-oz can frozen limeade concentrate, defrosted
1 6-oz can frozen lemonade concentrate, defrosted
1 6-oz can frozen orange juice concentrate, defrosted
Dry white wine
Carbonated water
Orange, lemon, or lime slices

1 In a small airtight container, combine all 3 frozen juice concentrates. Refrigerate until ready to use, for up to 2 weeks.
2 For an individual serving, mix 3 tablespoons juice mixture, ⅓ cup dry white wine, and ⅓ cup carbonated water in a tall glass. To serve, fill glass with ice and garnish with orange, lemon, or lime slices.
Yield: 12 servings

Vanna's White Wheels

Vanna eats! When Vanna wants a quick snack that doesn't muss what she's wearing tonight, she might enjoy these delicate, bite-size citrus circles. Rumor has it that she keeps a stock of them behind each letter she turns.

Preparation time: 15 minutes
Shaping and baking time: 30 minutes

> *¾ lb butter, softened*
> *1 cup confectioners' sugar*
> *3 cups all-purpose flour*
> *½ tsp salt*
> *2 tsps grated lemon rind*
> *½ tsp vanilla*
> *Granulated sugar*

1 With an electric beater, cream butter and confectioners' sugar until light and fluffy.

2 In a separate bowl, sift flour and salt together. Fold into butter-and-sugar mixture.

3 Add lemon rind and vanilla. Mix well. Chill several hours or overnight.

4 Preheat oven to 325°.

5 When ready to bake, roll dough on a floured surface to a ⅜-inch thickness. Using a 3-inch cookie cutter, cut out cookies. Sprinkle with granulated sugar and place on greased cookie sheet.

6 Bake for 20 minutes. Do not allow cookies to brown. Cool on a wire rack.

Yield: 2 dozen cookies

PLEDGE-DRIVE SPECIALS

Couch Potato epicures can take advantage of a food preparation time slot unique to public television: the pledge-drive break. Don't be annoyed when an especially tense moment in "The Jewel in the Crown" is interrupted by toothy local celebrities pointing to three pitiful telephone operators standing by dead phones and asking for your support or when the blue-chip stock market quotes on "Wall Street Week" are delayed by Alistair Cooke wheezing about how public television "depends on you." Instead, rush to your kitchen and use the time to whip up one of our "Pledge-Drive Specials."

Public television viewers have a long attention span, honed by practices such as watching the entire life cycle of the tsetse fly on "Nature" or waiting for Miss Marple to stop knitting on "Mystery!" This means they have the stamina to spend more time in the kitchen. We estimate that the average pledge-drive break lasts approximately 12 minutes—much longer than a station break. Use this opportunity to prepare these genteel and exotic recipes, which gracefully complement the type of programming usually found on public television.

For example, when a new "Masterpiece Theatre" production begins, what could be better than indulging in one of our Masterpiece Sundaes with a rich homemade fudge or a raspberry-chocolate sauce? For the confirmed Anglophile, we have a teatime repast that would tempt Victoria herself. Fortify yourself during those earnest, information-laden shows like "The MacNeil/Lehrer NewsHour" with a Sincere Open-Faced Ham with Brie(ding). With our "Pledge-Drive Specials," you can cultivate your palate as well as your mind.

Marple Mushroom Broil

Mushrooms are frequently the suspected murder weapons in English country estate mysteries, such as those Miss Marple solves. The only thing suspect about this mushroom sandwich is how something that takes so little time to fix can taste so delectable.

Preparation time: 12 minutes

> *1 3-oz package cream cheese, softened*
> *1 egg yolk*
> *1 tsp white wine or Worcestershire sauce*
> *1 cup fresh mushrooms, or ½ cup*
>   *finely chopped*
> *Dash freshly ground pepper*
> *6 halves lightly toasted English muffins*

1 In a food processor, combine cream cheese, Worcestershire sauce or white wine, egg yolk, mushrooms, and pepper. Process until mushrooms are finely chopped. If preparing by hand, chop mushrooms and combine ingredients in a small bowl until well mixed.

2 Spread mushroom mixture on toasted muffins. Broil until bubbly, about 5 minutes. Serve immediately.

Note: Mushroom mixture can be prepared ahead and broiled just before serving.

Yield: 6 sandwiches

Sincere Open-Faced Ham with Brie(ding)

When you find that you need something more substantial during a drawing room scene, try this sandwich, with the delicate flavors of honey-smoked ham and Brie.

Preparation time: microwave oven—2 minutes
                            conventional oven—7 minutes

1 slice dark rye bread
1 tsp course-ground mustard
2 ozs Brie, sliced, with rind removed
2 slices honey-smoked ham

1 Spread bread with mustard, then with Brie.
2 Top sandwich with ham slices.
3 Place on a microwave-safe plate. Microwave on high until the cheese has melted, about 20 to 30 seconds. In a conventional oven, broil 4 inches from heat for 3 to 4 minutes.

Yield: 1 sandwich

Masterpiece Sundaes

This pair of sauce recipes transforms any ice cream into an artfully crafted sundae to savor during an episode of "David Copperfield" or "Buddenbrooks."

Homemade Mocha Fudge Sundae

This rich chocolate sauce can be whipped up while the pledge-drive pitchman tries to tempt you by offering a glow-in-the-dark coffee cup as a premium.
Preparation time: 8 minutes

> 2 tbs instant espresso powder
> ½ cup strong coffee, brewed
> 1 cup heavy cream
> 1½ cups sugar
> 1 cup unsweetened cocoa
> 4 tbs butter
> 1 tsp vanilla
> 2 scoops vanilla ice cream
> 2 tbs cashews
> Whipped cream

1 Combine all ingredients except last 4 in a small saucepan and bring to a boil over medium heat.
2 Boil for 2 minutes, stirring constantly.
3 Remove from the heat and stir in vanilla.
4 Place vanilla ice cream in dish. Pour sauce over ice cream and top with roasted cashews and whipped cream.
Yield: 2 cups of sauce, enough for 8 servings

Raspberry-Chocolate Sundae

This provides a tart change of pace from plain chocolate sundaes. Perhaps you should save it for that rare "Masterpiece Theatre" series *not* set in England.
Preparation time: 5 minutes

1 10-oz package frozen raspberries
  in syrup, defrosted
1 tb Kirsch
8 scoops bittersweet chocolate gelato
  or chocolate ice cream
Whipped cream
Sugar wafer cookies

1 Process raspberries, syrup, and Kirsch on high until smooth in a blender or food processor.
2 Sieve seeds, if desired.
3 Serve over chocolate gelato or ice cream. Garnish with whipped cream and sugar wafer cookie.
Yield: 4 servings

Brit-Watching on PBS

On the PBS channels it is clear that Britannia still rules the waves—the airwaves that is. The PBS British invasion of recent years has brought us "Poldark," "The Jewel in the Crown," "Upstairs, Downstairs," "Executive Stress," "Fawlty Towers," and a whole slew of sleuths, including that old darling, Rumpole. From the wonderful eccentrics of "Brideshead Revisited" to the down-and-dirty oddballs of "EastEnders," Brit-watching offers enough quaint quirks and vicarious refinement for the most devoted Anglophile Potato. For the Couch Potato who is feeling proper, there is nothing like a British series to keep the starch in the collar and the upper lip stiff.

Perhaps the difficulty of keeping that peculiar expression while eating is why the British are so fond of taking tea. (What else can you eat while not moving your lip?) We have adapted this very proper ritual for the more relaxed Couch Potato lifestyle, without sacrificing the gracious feeling of the ceremony. With Anglo-American Tea, Alistair's Cookies, and Sherlock's Scones your coffee table is fully equipped for an evening with the English.

Anglo-American Tea

Those exquisite costume dramas, with the over-stuffed, dark, yet curiously comfortable drawing rooms, always have the obligatory scene of painfully repressed feelings being ignored during tea. The heroine proves her mettle by pouring without spilling a drop, even though her heart is breaking and the wolf (or the Irish) is at the door. The only acceptable drink to sip while watching such a scene is, of course, tea.

To accommodate the demands of Couch Potato life, we give you a simplified method for preparing the quintessential English beverage. You need no corset, bustle, or starched collar. Dismiss the servants for the evening. Arrange the couch, recline, and think of England.

Preparation time: 8 minutes

5 tea bags of Earl Grey or Irish Breakfast tea
4 cups of water
Hot water for teapot

1 Warm teapot by filling with hot tap water. Put 4 cups of water on to boil in a teakettle.

2 When water in teakettle is at a roiling boil, empty teapot. Put teabags in pot. Bring teapot to stove and add boiling water immediately.

3 Let tea steep for 3 minutes. Remove tea bags and serve immediately.

Yield: 5 ¾-cup servings

Sherlock's Scones

The master sleuth's love for these tasty treats is no mystery. Scones are a classic teatime repast, served with sweet butter and marmalade.

Preparation time: 20 minutes
Baking time: 20 minutes

2 cups all-purpose flour
4 tsps baking powder
¼ cup sugar
½ tsp salt
⅓ cup butter, chilled
1 egg, beaten
½ cup milk
½ cup dried currants or raisins
2 tsps grated orange rind (optional)
1 egg white
Granulated sugar

1 Preheat oven to 425°.

2 Combine flour, baking powder, sugar, and salt.

3 Cut butter into flour mixture until mixture resembles a coarse meal.

4 In a separate bowl, beat egg and mix with milk, currants, or raisins, and orange rind, if desired.

5 Add milk mixture to flour mixture and blend with a fork until moistened.

6 Turn dough out onto a floured board and knead for 30 seconds. Shape into a ball and roll to a 1-inch thickness.

7 Cut with a 2½-inch round cookie cutter. Place on ungreased cookie sheet. Brush with a lightly beaten egg white and sprinkle with granulated sugar.

8 Bake for 20 minutes. Serve with butter and jam.

Yield: 8 to 10 scones

Alistair's Cookies

These cookies are a variation on the traditional gingersnaps and are wonderful paired with tea as well as milk. They are crisp, not too sweet, and have a spicy bite, like the best British wit.

Preparation time: 15 minutes
Baking time: 10 to 12 minutes per sheet

½ cup butter, softened
¾ cup sugar
1 egg
¼ cup molasses
2½ cups flour
2 tsps baking soda
1½ tsps ginger
½ tsp nutmeg
½ tsp ground cloves
¼ tsp salt

1 Preheat oven to 375°.

2 Mix butter, sugar, egg, and molasses in a large bowl until the butter is thoroughly creamed.

3 Blend in remaining ingredients.

4 Shape dough by rounded teaspoonfuls into balls. Place balls 3 inches apart on lightly greased cookie sheet.

5 Bake 10 to 12 minutes. Remove from sheet and cool on paper towels.

Yield: 4 dozen cookies

WAITING FOR "L.A. LAW"

In every Couch Potato's life there comes that dismal time when nothing on any channel will satisfy you. Your favorite program will be on soon, but not soon enough. Your heart pounds, your pupils dilate, anxiety increases . . . you're not sure you'll make it. This condition is known as "Waiting for 'L.A. Law.'"

No show since the 1979-1980 season of "Dallas" has offered as much gratification on as many levels as "L.A. Law." There are the sex symbols (in enough variety to please both EEOC and affirmative action programs), shiny BMWs and Mercedes, copious supplies of money, and plenty of *food*. To Couch Potato gourmets, the food of "L.A. Law" is the real reason for watching the show. The Venus Butterfly is small potatoes when compared to the gigantic lobsters, the linguine al pesto, the erotic sushi menu, and the platters of fresh fruit, danish, and New York–style bagels that adorn every staff meeting.

Now you can deliver yourself from the trauma of waiting for your favorite show *and* enjoy the finest of L.A. lawyerly cuisine with our "Waiting for 'L.A. Law'" specialties. Each of these recipes can be prepared within 30 minutes: that may seem a long time, but we view it as a chance to save yourself from any uninteresting program that precedes "L.A. Law." (We won't suggest which shows to skip—one Couch Potato's lumps are another's au gratin.)

Once the show starts, you'll feel right at home with your "L.A. Law" Couch Potato delicacies. The dense, chewy Valencia Orange Shortbread will be a welcome diversion from Douglas Brackman's early morning directives, while the hearty Closed Case Sandwich is perfect for a quick bite before the 2:00 reconvening in court. For more romantic scenes, like the next time Stuart prepares one of his gourmet spreads for Ann, indulge in Stuart's Grecian Isles Salad. Try some of the cool and sensuous Grace's Frozen Champagne Grapes when she and Micky decorate the Christmas tree. Offer unlucky-in-love Victor a dish from the "Foods for Watching Alone" section of this book and wish him better luck next episode.

L.A. Slaw

What Gregory Peck did for white shirts in the 1950s, Arnie Becker does for ties in the 1980s. He has taken a tired staple of the businessman's wardrobe and infused it with virility. There are no wimpy yellows or cautious maroon-and-navy rep stripes in his tie wardrobe—his collection is a kaleidoscope of cerise, indigo, heliotrope, and flame. Need we say more than that our tart, multicolored L.A. Slaw was inspired by Arnie's fearless sartorial splendor? Red cabbage never looked so sexy.

Preparation time: 15 minutes

2 cups shredded white cabbage
2 cups shredded red cabbage
1 cup peeled, shredded carrots
½ cup diced green pepper
½ cup diced red pepper
4 green onions, thinly sliced
⅓ cup tarragon vinegar
¼ cup sugar
1 tb Dijon mustard
Salt and pepper to taste
¾ cup olive oil

1 Combine vegetables in a large bowl. (To save time, process vegetables in a food processor.)

2 In a separate bowl, combine all remaining ingredients except oil. Whisk in oil, a little at a time, until dressing thickens. A food processor or blender at high speed can also be used.

3 Toss vegetables with dressing to taste. Refrigerate until ready to serve.

Yield: 6 servings

Stuart's Grecian Isles Salad

When Stuart wants to whisk Ann away for a week on Corfu, but can't break away from work, he prepares a romantic Greek dinner at home, beginning with this heady salad of pasta, feta cheese, and black olives. If he serves this lusty dish with Greek ouzo, he and Ann usually move the second course into the boudoir.

Preparation time: 20 minutes

8 ozs shell pasta
⅓ cup olive oil
1 large ripe tomato, peeled, seeded, and diced
½ cup pitted Greek olives
1 small cucumber, peeled, seeded, and sliced
8 ozs feta cheese, cubed
Salt and coarsely ground pepper to taste
2 tbs chopped fresh parsley

1 Cook pasta according to package directions. Drain well.

2 Toss pasta with all remaining ingredients. Serve immediately.

Yield: 2 to 4 servings

Peppered Torts

When you are exhausted from an evening of vicarious ambulance-chasing, this tortellini pasta is the perfect pick-me-up. After serving this dish, the only complaint the chef will hear is of insufficient amounts for third helpings.

Preparation time: 25 minutes

1 cup dried, cheese-filled tortellini
2 cups red and green pepper strips
½ lb cooked, smoked sausage, diagonally sliced
2 tbs unsalted butter
1 tb flour
¾ cup milk
1 cup shredded Swiss cheese
2 tsps Dijon mustard

1 In a large pot, cook tortellini in boiling salted water until tender, about 12 minutes. Drain and set aside.

2 While the pasta is cooking, sauté peppers and sausage in 1 tablespoon butter in a skillet. Cook until peppers are tender but still crisp. Remove and set aside.

3 Wipe skillet clean. Melt remaining butter over medium heat. Stir in flour to form a paste.

4 Slowly add milk, stirring constantly, until mixture thickens. Add cheese and mustard. Continue to stir until cheese melts.

5 Add tortellini, peppers, and sausage. Serve immediately.

Yield: 4 servings

Cheesy Potato Briefs

If you time this right, these crisp potato snacks will be ready to take from the oven while the "Previously on L.A. Law" clips air. They will be cool enough to eat by the time you find out who's taking advantage of Douglas Brackman this week.

Preparation time: 25 minutes

> 2 medium baking potatoes, unpeeled and
>   sliced, ¼-inch thick
> 2 tbs butter, melted
> ½ tsp paprika
> 1 clove garlic, minced
> Salt and pepper to taste
> ¼ cup Parmesan cheese

1 Preheat oven to 375°.
2 Place potato slices in single layer on greased baking sheet.
3 Combine butter and seasonings in small bowl. Brush over potato slices. Sprinkle with cheese.
4 Bake for 20 minutes or until crisp.
Yield: 2 servings

Closed Case Sandwich

For afternoon staff meetings, this herbed roast-beef nosh is a natural. Its simple elegance makes it the ideal counterpart for the more flamboyant L.A. Slaw (see page 37).

Preparation time: 10 minutes

HERB SPREAD

1 clove garlic
1 slice onion
1 8-oz package cream cheese, softened
½ cup unsalted butter, softened
¼ cup chopped parsley
Salt and coarse ground pepper to taste

SANDWICH

4 croissants, split
Alfalfa sprouts
8 ozs rare roast beef, sliced

1 To make the herb spread, combine first 6 ingredients in a food processor. Process until mixture is smooth. Refrigerate until ready to serve.

2 Spread split croissants with herb spread. Top with sprouts and roast-beef slices. Wrap in plastic wrap and refrigerate until the show begins.

Yield: 4 servings

Grace's Frozen Champagne Grapes

This snack cheats a little bit—it takes longer than 30 minutes for the grapes to freeze properly and it is something of an exaggeration to call it a recipe. Still, frozen grapes are the perfect treat for an ice princess like Grace: they are cool, elegant, and sweet, and you don't have to get your hands dirty to prepare them.

Preparation time: 5 minutes
Freezing time: 24 hours

1 large bunch of champagne or other fresh grapes

1 Wash grapes and remove stems. Place grapes in plastic bag or container, close tightly and keep in freezer overnight. Serve in glass bowl.

Yield: 1 bunch

Victor's Sangria Spritzer

One of the mysteries of "L.A. Law" is how Douglas Brackman can have a decent woman (literally) fall at his feet while Victor Sifuentes attracts only husband-killers and man-eating dentists. We're sure that someday Victor will meet a good woman. When he does, the two can celebrate their first evening together with this bubbly sangria.

Preparation time: 10 minutes

½ cup orange juice
¼ cup lemon juice
½ cup sugar
1⅘-quart bottle Sangria or dry red wine
1 7-oz bottle club soda
1 cup sliced fruits (any combination of
   oranges, apples, lemons)
Ice

1 Pour the juices and sugar into a 2½-quart serving pitcher. Stir to dissolve sugar.

2 Add wine, soda, and fruit just before serving. Pour into tall glasses, making sure each serving has a mix of fruit.

Yield: 6 to 8 servings

Valencia Orange Shortbread

Like so many of today's hot items, such as analog watches, this recipe takes an old favorite, Scottish shortbread, and adds a new twist to give it a contemporary flair. Freshly squeezed orange juice and whole wheat flour give these cookies a chewy texture and subtle taste as retro-cool as Arnie's French-cuffed white shirts.

Preparation time: 15 minutes
Baking time: 25 to 30 minutes

¼ cup freshly squeezed orange juice
¾ cup unsalted butter
⅓ cup sugar
¼ tsp salt
2 cups white or whole wheat flour

1 Preheat oven to 350°.

2 Squeeze oranges. (For ¼ cup juice, use 2 small Valencia oranges or 1 large navel orange.) Strain juice and set aside.

3 Cream butter, sugar, and salt together.

4 Work 1 cup of flour into butter mixture with fingers or pastry blender. Add juice slowly with the second cup of flour.

5 Roll out dough on greased and floured cookie sheet about ½-inch thick. Cut dough into rectangles. Bake for about 25 to 30 minutes or until golden brown.

Yield: 3 dozen cookies

LATE-NIGHT VIEWING

It's been a long evening of prime time—clandestine trysts, multimillion-dollar swindles, and reckless car chases. You need to unwind from all the excitement and ease into late-night viewing.

Beginning with the closing theme of the late-night news and ending with "The Star-Spangled Banner," these viewing hours are a time of reflection and relaxation. Old friends (Johnny, Ted, David, the Kramdens, the crew of the original *Enterprise*) drop by for a snack and a soothing word or chuckle.

This tranquil reliability is what we bring to the recipes for the late-night hours. In these dishes, there are no surprising spice combinations or acquired tastes. Our "Midnight Comfort Food" snacks and drinks are so calming and familiar that they might have appeared on your grandmother's kitchen table or in the back of her liquor cabinet. The "Reruns" recipes could have been served at some of our favorite characters' suppers. And anyone who has stolen into the kitchen at 4 A.M. for a peanut-butter-and-pickle sandwich will recognize our "Foor for Watching Alone" specialties.

These "Late-Night Viewing" foods are meant to help you end your day in peace. If you're an insomniac, they will lull you to sleep; if you're nervous, they will soothe you; if you have a secret food fantasy, they will indulge you. After all, you need to be refreshed for another day of viewing.

MIDNIGHT COMFORT FOOD

These hours, which run from the tinkle of "The Tonight Show" theme to the close of "The David Letterman Show," mark the first crucial step into the late-night viewing hours. As a tired but wired Tuber, you need something to get you started on the road to slumber. Johnny's easygoing monologue and Ted Koppel's neatly coiffed hair contribute to your calm, but you need more. Each of these Midnight Comfort Foods is designed to rid you of the worries and frustrations of the day. Koppel Cocoa will calm you; Here's Johnnycakes will bring out the kid in you; Letterman's Spiked Cider will mellow you; Test Pattern Toddy will rouse you for "The Star-Spangled Banner." All are sure to cure you of any mental trauma sustained while watching the late-night newscast.

Here's Johnnycakes

"The Tonight Show" is an American institution—Johnny Carson has probably eased more people into sleep than Brahms's lullaby. This is not the traditional Johnnycake recipe; it's a fritter batter that allows you to substitute apples for the corn on the nights when Jay Leno is the guest host. Fritters are best served drenched in syrup or molasses to satisfy that midnight sweet tooth.

Preparation time: 10 minutes
Frying time: 10 to 15 minutes

1¾ cups flour
3 tsps baking powder
½ tsp salt
1 egg, slightly beaten
1 cup milk
1 tsp melted butter, cooled
2 cups fresh corn or drained canned corn
Oil for frying
Maple syrup or molasses to taste

1 Sift dry ingredients together into a bowl. Begin heating enough oil for deep-fat frying in frying pan.
2 Mix milk, egg, and butter together, and pour into flour mixture. Stir until smooth.
3 Add corn and stir until well mixed.
4 Drop by tablespoonfuls into deep hot oil. Fry for 3 to 5 minutes until evenly brown. Turn fritters as they rise to the surface of the oil. Drain on paper towels.
5 Drizzle syrup over fritters and serve.
Yield: 6 servings of 4 or 5 fritters each

Jay Leno Guest Host Fritters

Jay Leno is just as wholesome as Johnny himself, so if you can't have Nebraska corn, all-American apples are the next best thing. Follow the Here's Johnnycakes recipe as indicated, except substitute corn with:

2 cups chopped apples
1 tb sugar

Koppel Cocoa

This soothing "Nightline" elixir keeps you calm during those pesky three-way satellite hookups and unflappable through interviews with slippery foreign embassy officials. It eases the transition from the day's nasty events to a good night's sleep.

Preparation time: 5 minutes

>
> *⅓ cup unsweetened cocoa*
> *⅓ cup sugar*
> *½ cup boiling water*
> *3½ cups milk*
> *1 tsp vanilla*
> *Marshmallows or marshmallow cream*

1 In a blender container, combine cocoa, sugar, and boiling water.

2 Cover and blend at low speed until sugar is dissolved.

3 In a small pot, warm milk and vanilla over low heat. Be careful not to scald milk.

4 Add warmed milk and vanilla to cocoa mixture in the blender. Process until frothy.

5 Serve immediately and garnish with a marshmallow or a tablespoon of marshmallow cream.

Yield: 4 8-oz servings

Letterman's Spiked Cider

After the excitement of yet another stupid pet trick, Letterman's Spiked Cider is just the right thing to sip. The hot mug warms your fingers, the spices tickle your nose, and the brandy makes David seem friendly as well as funny.

Preparation time: 20 minutes

>
> *½ cup brown sugar*
> *1 tsp whole allspice*
> *1 tsp whole cloves*

Dash ground nutmeg
4-inch stick cinnamon
2 qts apple cider
½ cup apple brandy
  (Calvados or applejack)
Orange slices

1 In a large Dutch oven or pot, combine the first 6 ingredients. Bring to a gentle boil.
2 Cover and simmer 15 minutes.
3 Remove from heat. Stir in brandy and orange slices.
4 Serve in mugs.
Yield: 8 servings

Test Pattern Toddy

To a Couch Potato, there are no sadder words than, "This station now ends its broadcast day." Night after night, it's a slap in the face of your loyalty. What you really deserve is a reward for your perfect attendance.

That's why we created our Test Pattern Toddy. This smooth mix of whiskey, orange, and cinnamon will warm your tummy, yet provide the kick you need to get into bed. Nurse it through "Sermonette" or raise it in toast to "The Star-Spangled Banner."

Preparation time: 6 minutes

1 jigger Scotch whiskey
1 tsp sugar
1 cinnamon stick
6 ozs boiling water
Thin orange wedge
Dash of crushed cloves

1 Place whiskey and sugar in mug and stir with cinnamon stick.
2 Add boiling water. Stir again. Top with orange wedge and dust with cloves. Serve immediately.
Yield: 1 serving

Rerun Treats

The characters in reruns are the most dependable friends in the world. They don't cancel dinner plans at the last minute or flirt with your boyfriend. They've stayed with you through your "Wonder Years" and through the "thirtysomething" decade.

To honor these stalwart friends, we've created these special "Reruns" recipes. Each of these dishes could have shown up on the rerun that inspired it. Sue Ann Nivens of "The Mary Tyler Moore Show" would have enjoyed the flavor (and the alliteration) of our Hearty Happy Homemaker Muffins, and the Skipper might have had more respect for his first mate if he had prepared Gilligan's Mock Minnow Stew. Our Odd Couple Heroes capture the "Jekyll and Hyde" food sensibilities of TV's most mismatched twosome. Our black-and-white Rerun Treats are just as fitting. All of the foods, from Beaver Cleaver's Brownie à la Mode to Ricky Ricardo's Cuban Coffee to the Honeymooners' Munch Mix, contain only dark and light ingredients: we would never colorize a classic show with bright nouvelle cuisine.

You'll also appreciate the variety of preparation times. Some recipes are so simple that they can be prepared during Craftmatic Bed and Time-Life Record commercials. For those that take longer, remember that it's not as crucial that you catch all the lines anyway, since you've probably committed them to memory.

Odd Couple Heroes

When Felix didn't have the time to prepare Beef Wellington, he snacked on the finest sliced meats dotted with Dusseldorf mustard on crusty French bread. When Oscar was late on a deadline, he downed two hot dogs from a street vendor for dinner and saved the rolls for a midnight snack with the pound of bologna he bought two weeks ago.

Since most of us have a combination of Oscar and Felix's culinary tastes, we've assembled both characters' favorite meats, cheeses, condiments, and breads in the following list, so you can prepare your own Odd Couple Hero. Felix stored a few of these sandwiches in his freezer for picnics; Oscar left several half-eaten ones in his bed.

Preparation time: 5 to 10 minutes, depending on size of sandwich

1 Choose 3 from column F and 3 from column O and assemble sandwich.

2 Close your eyes and eat.

Yield: 1 sandwich

COLUMN F	COLUMN O
Prosciutto	Beer Salami
Smoked salmon	Liverwurst
Mesquite-smoked turkey breast	Corned beef
Camembert	Pastrami
Danish Havarti	
Double Gloucester	Head cheese
	Velveeta
	American cheese
Roasted red pepper strips	Bermuda onions
Red leaf lettuce	Dill pickles
Plum tomatoes	Iceberg lettuce
Dijon mustard	Ketchup
Dusseldorf mustard	Yellow mustard
Homemade mayonnaise	Bottled salad dressing (any kind)
French bread	Submarine rolls
Black bread	Hot dog rolls

Trekkie Trail Mix

As Sulu and Chekhov settle behind their 23rd century consoles and peer into the vastness of space, an alien noise rocks the ship. Uhura taps her mike. Spock arches an eyebrow. The red alert sirens go wild. Kirk leaps to his feet. "Go back to your stations!" he shouts. "Remain calm! We are not under attack!" He lifts his bowl of Trekkie Trail Mix, an exotic blend of ship-style dried fruit and "warp factor" mini-pretzels. "The strange noise you heard was my crunching," he says. He turns to McCoy: "Bones—give me a nutritional reading on this." McCoy scowls, "I'm a doctor, not a dietician." Trail mix rations are distributed to the crew, who go on to boldly crunch where no man has crunched before.

Preparation time: 10 minutes

⅔ cup dried apples, cut into small bits
⅔ cup banana chips
⅔ cup dark raisins
2 cups mini-pretzels
1 cup dry roasted peanuts
Cinnamon to taste

1 Mix together all ingredients in large bowl and dust with cinnamon.
2 Store leftovers in plastic containers.
Yield: 4 to 6 servings

"M★A★S★H" Hash

The members of the 4077 had many creative responses to the mystery food Igor served up on the chow line. We bet the quips would have been kinder if he had had our recipe for "M*A*S*H" Hash.

Preparation time: 20 minutes

6 tbs butter
1 large onion, chopped
2 medium potatoes, cooked and cubed
3 cups cooked, cubed roast beef
2 tbs freshly minced parsley
½ tsp thyme
Dash of red pepper sauce
Salt and pepper to taste

1 In a skillet, melt 2 tablespoons butter over medium heat.

2 Sauté onion until lightly browned, about 10 minutes. Remove to a bowl and toss with potatoes, beef, and seasonings.

3 Melt remaining 4 tablespoons butter. Spread meat and potato mixture over skillet bottom. Cook until bottom is crusty.

Yield: 6 servings

Gilligan's Mock Minnow Stew

Everyone's favorite castaways were seldom seen to eat anything. They were too busy trying to be rescued or coping with kooky visitors on what must have been TV's busiest desert isle. Gilligan and his friends had more guests than "Fantasy Island." In memory of the Skipper's beloved ship, try our Gilligan's Mock Minnow Stew, a creamy chowder topped with crunchy fish-shape crackers.

Preparation time: 20 minutes

6 slices bacon, diced
¼ cup chopped onion
2 cups cubed potatoes
2 cups hot water
1½ lbs cod, cut into chunks
2 cups cream
Chopped parsley
Salt and freshly ground pepper to taste
Pepperidge Farm® Cheddar Cheese
  Goldfish

1 In a skillet, cook bacon until almost crisp.
2 Add onion and sauté until tender. Drain excess fat.
3 Add potatoes and water. Cover and simmer until potatoes are almost tender, about 5 minutes.
4 Add cod and continue to cook covered until fish flakes with a fork, about 3 minutes.
5 Stir in cream, heat through. Season with salt and pepper.
6 Garnish with parsley and Cheddar Cheese Goldfish.
Yield: 4 to 6 servings

Hearty Happy Homemaker Muffins

Sue Ann Nivens, the scheming host of WJM's "Happy Homemaker Show," seemed to have only two goals in life: to capture Lou Grant and to beat Chuckles the Clown in the ratings. If she had prepared these hearty muffins, she might have accomplished both.

Preparation time: 8 minutes
Baking time: 15 minutes

3 cups bran flakes
1¼ cups all-purpose flour
⅓ cup sugar
1¼ tsps baking soda
¼ tsp salt
1 egg
1 cup buttermilk
¼ cup vegetable oil
½ cup raisins

1 Preheat oven to 400°.
2 In a bowl, combine the bran flakes, flour, sugar, baking soda, and salt.
3 In a separate bowl, beat egg, buttermilk, and oil.
4 Gently stir egg mixture and raisins into flour mixture. Do not overmix. Refrigerate batter, if desired, until ready to bake.
5 Spoon mixture into greased muffin pan, filling ¾ full.
6 Bake 15 minutes or until lightly browned. Remove immediately and cool on a wire rack.

Yield: 15 2½-inch muffins

Honeymooners' Munch Mix

Every night following the late news, millions of TV viewers eschew comic monologues for the antics of Ralph, Ed, Alice, and Trixie. The same 39 shows from the classic 1955–1956 season of "The Honeymooners" have aired in reruns for years, and there is no sign of stopping.

In one famous episode, when Ralph and Ed buy a TV, Ralph spreads a shopping bag full of snacks over the table, stares at the TV, and starts eating. Now you can join Ralph with the Honeymooners Munch Mix, a spicy snack made of chow mein noodles from their favorite restaurant, the Hong Kong Gardens. Simple and satisfying, this treat may surpass even the infamous KramMar's Delicious Mystery Appetizer.

Preparation time: 17 minutes

4 tbs butter or margarine, melted
1 tsp Worcestershire sauce
1 tsp garlic salt
1 tsp seasoned salt
1 3-oz can chow mein noodles

1 Preheat oven to 250°.
2 Combine all ingredients except noodles.
3 Place noodles on a baking pan. Drizzle butter mixture over noodles and toss.
4 Toast in oven about 15 minutes.
Yield: 2½ cups

Beaver Cleaver's Brownie à la Mode

In an early (now lost) episode of "Leave It to Beaver," TV history was made when Eddie Haskell spied this classic chocolate delicacy on the Cleaver kitchen table and uttered the fateful compliment, "Why, Mrs. Cleaver, how lovely you look today."

Preparation time: 5 minutes
Baking time: 25 minutes

2 1-oz squares unsweetened chocolate
½ cup butter or margarine
2 eggs
1 cup sugar
1 tsp vanilla
½ cup flour
1 cup chopped pecans
Vanilla ice cream
Fudge sauce

1 Preheat oven to 350°.
2 Melt chocolate and butter in saucepan over low heat. Set aside.
3 Beat eggs. Add sugar and vanilla, and stir. Stir in melted chocolate mixture, flour, and nuts.
4 Bake in a greased 9-inch pie pan for 25 minutes, until the top is crusty.
5 To serve, slice warm brownie and top with rich vanilla ice cream and fudge sauce, if desired.
Yield: 9 servings

Ricky Ricardo's Cuban Coffee

Keeping up with Lucy's antics requires both alertness and steady nerves. Our Ricky Ricardo's Cuban Coffee can help with both: caffeine to perk you up when Lucy begins her explanation of the latest disaster, and rum to calm you down when she's through.

Preparation time: 1 minute

> *1 cup strong coffee*
> *2 tsps molasses*
> *1 tb rum*

1 Pour cup of hot coffee, add molasses and rum, and stir.

Yield: 1 serving

FOOD FOR WATCHING ALONE

The Couch Potato gourmet is as discriminating a diner as he is a viewer and generally prepares food to complement the television agenda. There are occasional conflicts with friends or mates over which dip goes best with which chip or the choice of the evening's viewing, but on the whole Couch Potato life is spent in harmony, being amused and fed in the company of loved ones. Once in a while, however, a Couch Potato will have an evening alone, with no one to fight with for the remote control unit or the last of the guacamole.

Savvy Spuds see this evening for what it really is: an opportunity to escape *food shame*. This is not the shame that comes from refusing to clear your plate and offering to send your untouched liver and Brussels sprouts to starving children in India. It is the shame that comes from not eating culinarily fashionable, politically correct, and nutritionally balanced food. An evening alone offers the opportunity to indulge in treasured but misunderstood cravings for special foods. These cravings can range from small social rebellions, such as a loyalty to Brie while everyone else favors Holland Gouda, to major regressions such as a passion for Fluffernutter or Nestlé's Quik straight from the can. It could be a lust for liverwurst, onion, and anchovy sandwiches, a combination that turns your favorite couch buddy slightly green. When viewing alone, the social niceties can be discarded, freeing you to concoct dishes that no one would confess to eating in public. Best of all, you don't have to share.

When you want to expand your repertoire of forbidden favorites, here is a collection of recipes that give new meaning to the words *secret self-indulgence*. We have collected recipes from a number of sources, all of whom swear that these concoctions are actually edible and dear to their hearts. To protect the reputations of those involved, some of the names have been withheld.

In honor of all those times when you ate what was on your plate instead of what you secretly wanted, we give you "Food for Watching Alone." Most of these recipes are for one or two servings; after all, they are just for you.

Pickle-Peanut Butter-Cheese Rolls

A renowned Chicago art consumer we know eats these treats while watching *film noir* on her VCR. "Buy the individually wrapped cheese food singles," she says. "They're the only kind that provides the right sweetness. And don't skimp on the peanut butter."

Preparation time: 6 minutes

> 1 Kaiser roll, split in half
> 1 tb peanut butter
> 2 individually wrapped slices American cheese
> 1 large dill pickle, sliced

1 Spread both sides of roll with peanut butter.
2 Add cheese and pickles. Close sandwich and eat.

Yield: 1 sandwich

Pink Devil Tea Sandwiches

A California caterer we know originally thought that her deviled ham-cream cheese mixture was too outré for her food-buying public. But one day she paired her Pink Devil spread with store-bought white bread and cut the sandwiches into favorite TV-watching shapes, and her business boomed. Her favorite tea sandwich shapes are hearts (for "Love Boat") and diamonds (for "Dynasty").

Preparation time: 10 minutes

6 ozs canned deviled ham spread
6 ozs cream cheese
8 slices white bread

1 Blend deviled ham spread and cream cheese.
2 Spread on 4 slices of bread and top with remaining 4 slices.
3 Cut into desired shapes with cookie cutters.
Yield: 8 to 12 sandwiches

Tempeh-Peanut Butter Melt

This is made by a vegetarian friend of ours, who swears by it as a healthy and tasty treat. At this writing, he has yet to persuade anyone else to eat it, so it seemed to fit here.
Preparation time: 8 minutes

1 slice whole grain pita bread
1 thin slice of tempeh or other pressed soy
   food product
1 tb peanut butter
1 slice low-fat cheese
Soy sauce

1 Spread the peanut butter on the slice of pita bread. Put the tempeh slice on top, score it with a knife, and add soy sauce to taste. The scoring helps the soy sauce soak in better. Top with slice of cheese.
2 Place under the broiler for 3 to 5 minutes or until cheese is melted. Serve immediately.
Yield: 1 serving.

Ketchup Sandwich

When a famous Midwestern tycoon we know comes home after a rough day of attempted takeovers, she consoles herself with this favorite sandwich from her childhood. She enjoys it while watching Johnny Carson.

Preparation time: 2 minutes

> *2 slices white bread (with crusts to fence in ketchup)*
> *Ketchup to taste*

1 Place ketchup in middle of 1 slice of bread.
2 Top with other slice of bread and squeeze. Do not cut sandwich into halves.

Yield: 1 sandwich

Chocolade Hagel Sandwich

Chocolade hagel means "chocolate hail" in Dutch and looks like little chocolate sprinkles. To the casual observer, Dutch chocolade hagel might be confused with American chocolate "Jimmies," but this is like comparing the work of Van Gogh to a finger painting in Mrs. Streets' kindergarten class. Hagel normally comes in "melk chocolade" or "puur chocolade." It can be found in European food specialty stores or through De Wildt Imports, Inc.

Preparation time: 4 minutes

1 slice bread (brown bread preferred)
Unsalted butter to taste
Chocolade hagel to taste

1 Bread can be toasted or untoasted, brown bread is best. Slice bread to desired thickness.

2 Spread on desired layer of country-fresh butter (margarine will *not* do) and sprinkle on a hearty layer of hagel. Be neither too sparing nor too immoderate.

Yield: 1 serving

Marshmallow Cheese Toast

This is a truly misunderstood and maligned treat. The mere mention of it brings looks of dismay to cultured faces. But it is sweet and cheesy and crunchy all at once: what more could you want from a snack food?

Preparation time: 8 minutes

4 slices of toasted white bread
4 slices of American cheese
16 large marshmallows

1 On a cookie sheet arrange slices of toast. On each slice put 1 slice of cheese.

2 Top with 4 marshmallows. Make sure that the edges of the bread are not touching so that the marshmallows will not melt together across the slices.

3 Place in oven under the broiler for 3 to 4 minutes, until the marshmallows have a light brown crust on top, but are still holding their shape.

4 Serve hot.

Yield: 4 servings

Flaky Peanut Butter Dips

An avid Midwestern birdwatching friend enjoys this quick cornflakes-and-peanut butter breakfast at 5:30 A.M., while planning her day's TV and birdwatching agendas. Rice Krispies are also a good accompaniment to peanut butter.

Preparation time: 1 minute

> *1 12-oz jar peanut butter (any style)*
> *1 12-oz box cornflakes*

1 Dip butter knife in peanut butter and extract large slab.
2 Place peanut butter–covered knife into cornflakes. Cover thoroughly.
3 Remove and eat. Repeat process as often as desired.
Yield: 1 serving

Bird Seed

New York City tennis champion Rick Starr calls Bird Seed "the most delicious high-class junk food" he knows. "I eat it when I think of it," he says. To refresh his memory (and introduce you to this delicacy), here is his recipe.

Preparation time: 3 minutes

> *Equal parts of the following:*
> *Plain M&Ms*
> *Salted peanuts*
> *Raisins*
> *Sugar Smacks*

1 Mix all ingredients and serve in large bowl.
Yield: 1 serving

Single-Note Pig Outs

There are a sizeable number of Spuds who choose not to prepare their own "Food for Watching Alone," but would rather eat one commercially prepared food in astonishing quantity. These are the "Single-Noters," for whom the old Lay's Potato Chip slogan, "Bet You Can't Eat Just One," refers to one bag, not one chip.

Those who indulge in "Single-Note Pig Outs" usually fall into three categories: the Fast-Track Gobblers, the Food Wimps, and the Purists.

Fast-Track Gobblers believe that more is more and faster is better. They look at food from the Bottom Line: preparing a pickle-peanut-butter-cheese sandwich simply takes too much time. It is more efficient and more enjoyable to eat each food separately in quick succession. Fast-Track Gobblers consider themselves street-smart and highly organized about food, and they disapprove of people who delay gratification by "preparing a snack." Fast-trackers often also enjoy quick entertainment, such as 15-second commercials and five-card stud.

Food Wimps have never shed their food shame. Not only are they reluctant to order bologna on white bread in public, they are just as timid alone. To overcome their phobia, they will buy several small packages of their favorite snacks, telling themselves they will eat in moderation. Eight two-ounce packs of Raisinets later, they have consumed just as much as the more economical one-pound bag.

Purists are the snack-food aesthetes. Unlike Food Wimps, they feel no shame at eating an 18-ounce bag of Oreos, but refuse to touch them once they've been mixed into vanilla ice cream. It disrupts their sense of order. These people believe that food should be appreciated for its artistic value as well as enjoyed in large quantities. They have been known to arrange entire bags of plain M&Ms in Expressionistic collages before eating them.

Some of our favorite Single-Note Pig Outs include:

- entire cans or jars of peanuts
- entire boxes of cookies
- entire bags of potato chips
- entire jars of peanut butter

NOT CONFINED TO PRIME TIME

Although prime time continues to make up the bulk of the average Couch Potato's viewing schedule, the 1980s have seen the dawn of the Brave New World of Television. Recent technological advances have liberated Couch Potatoes from a steady diet of major network programming. Thanks to videocassette recorders, cable, and UHF, Couch Potatoes need never utter the dreaded words, "There's nothing to watch on TV."

With the exception of the remote control, the most essential high-tech TV tool is the VCR. Video stores have multiplied faster than hamburger joints across the American landscape, providing a vast array of movies and, for the terminally optimistic, countless self-improvement tapes. VCRs allow viewers to tape shows and watch at their convenience, making any time prime time. Shows that are inconsiderately scheduled, such as "The Bugs Bunny Show" on Saturday morning (a time when most normal Tubers are still asleep) can be savored at leisure. These amazing machines allow the viewer total timing control, which provides the opportunity for an expanded range of foods to be prepared without missing any important television moment. The benefits are clear: being able to bake your brownies and eat them too, without missing a punchline. The "VCR Intermission Specials" offer recipes that take advantage of this handy device.

High-tech also gives us cable and a bewildering array of new viewing options. Cable is truly TV for every taste, from the all-news networks to the health channel, from Home Box Office to MTV. To accommodate this range in choice, we have developed cable recipes from snacks for exercise buffs to MTV munchies. MTV is especially flexible, in that the viewer can still listen while preparing food in the kitchen, an experience that has a high nostalgia factor, given its similarity to radio.

With TV routinely offering 184-channel capabilities, UHF channels are also multiplying. In addition to distant PBS outlets, these channels also feature very targeted programming aimed at heretofore neglected audience segments. Spanish *novelas*, Texas-based "Bodywatch," and the inimitable Home Shopping Club are but three examples.

Freed from the constraints of prime-time programming, Couch Potato style can now be a 24-hour activity.

VCR INTERMISSION SPECIALS: WHEN THE TUBER GOES HOLLYWOOD

In the old days, movies had intermissions. After Scarlett O'Hara snatched a carrot from the devastated grounds of Tara and vowed, "As God is my witness, I'll never be hungry again," the word *Intermission* flashed on the screen, the drapes closed, and hundreds of hungry viewers ran to the candy counter. Intermission was the perfect time to stock up for the next reel.

Now that theaters have tightened their viewing schedules to bring in more money, intermissions have gone the way of Looney Tunes and Metrotone Newsreels. As a result, movie munchers have had to become fugitives, stealing away during what they hope will be a minor shootout or an inconsequential sex scene to fortify themselves for the movie's denouement. (Controversy still rages as to whether an intermission might have saved *Heaven's Gate*.)

Watching movies on TV has brought different, but no less troubling, frustrations. When your favorite movie finally did make it to TV, it was riddled with commercial breaks so short that they gave you time to do little more than grab another bag of potato chips. Movies with "limited commercial interruptions" were good for gourmet cooking, but only if you strategically planned your recipe to coincide with the station breaks.

Fortunately for Couch Potato movie buffs, the VCR has changed all that. It has restored dignity to the act of eating while viewing a film. With a VCR, Couch Potatoes can create their own intermissions, prepare foods to their heart's content, and not miss a minute of their favorite movies.

To celebrate this return to film-watching civility, we have created these "Intermission Specials," seven movie-inspired sandwiches and light supper entrées that can be prepared during your self-appointed intermissions. These delicacies are perfect for those Saturday nights or Sunday afternoons when you need just the right sustenance for a Japanese epic or a Cary Grant double bill.

For lovers of westerns, there is the spicy *Red River* Omelet Sandwich, a hearty mix of green peppers, eggs, and ham—just the dish Walter Brennan would have prepared for John Wayne if they hadn't been stranded on the Chisholm Trail. Mystery lovers will fancy Mr. Moto Takes a Snack, a spicy mix of tender beef and crisp broccoli. (Should you need a nosh between entrées, whip up some of the "Ode to Popcorn" treats we offer earlier in the book on pages 21-23.)

We feel confident that with these "VCR Intermission Specials" we have solved the most pressing Couch Potato movie lover's problem. Now we can move on to the next modern movie quandary. Whatever happened to necking?

Mr. Moto Takes a Snack

Think fast, Mr. Moto! This somewhat Oriental sandwich will help set the mood for the somewhat Oriental detective played by Peter Lorre. Charlie Chan would be proud of this spicy blend of beef, peppers, and garlic in a Chinese pancake. Rumor has it Mr. Moto developed this recipe between crimes on Danger Island.

Preparation time: 10 minutes
Cooking time: 2½ to 3 minutes

3 tbs sesame oil
1 clove garlic, minced
1 tsp fresh ginger root, minced
¾ lb beef flank steak, cut across the grain into paper-thin strips
1 green and 1 red pepper, seeded and cut into thin strips
3 tbs soy sauce
2 tsps cornstarch
4 large flour tortillas, Chinese pancakes, or pitas, warmed

1 Heat oil in skillet. Combine all ingredients except tortillas, pancakes, or pitas in the skillet.
2 Stir-fry meat mixture until meat loses its redness and sauce thickens.
3 Top each tortilla or pancake with ¼ of the mixture and wrap envelope-style or stuff into pitas.
Yield: 4 servings

Red River Omelet Sandwiches

John Wayne and his men got pretty tired of boiled beans on their long cattle drive across the Chisholm Trail. This classic egg sandwich was one of the restaurant's biggest sellers when the cattlemen finally brought their herd through town. Real men *do* eat omelets.

Preparation time: 8 minutes

2 tbs butter or margarine
½ cup diced cooked ham
¼ medium green pepper, diced
½ small onion, diced
3 large eggs
1 tb milk
¼ tsp salt
Pepper to taste
4 slices whole wheat bread, toasted
Mild or spicy bottled salsa (optional)

1 In a frying pan, melt butter over medium heat. Sauté ham, green pepper, and onion until tender.

2 Meanwhile, in a mixing bowl, beat eggs, milk, and seasonings. Pour into heated skillet over ham, pepper, and onion. Turn heat to low and cook until eggs are set and lightly browned on the bottom.

3 Cut the egg omelet in half and serve each portion between toasted bread slices. Add salsa, if desired.

Yield: 2 servings

Annie Hall West Burger

Aside from right turns on red, California had little to offer Alvy Singer, but this sandwich might have changed all that. He might even have been able to lure Annie back from L.A. if their favorite New York deli had offered this hearty hamburger topped with avocado, tomatoes, and Monterey Jack. The burger is equally good while watching the Knicks in your bedroom or when hiding from the spider that's ransacking the bathroom.

Preparation time: 10 minutes

1 lb lean ground beef
Salt and pepper to taste
4 slices Monterey Jack cheese
1 medium tomato, sliced
4 lettuce leaves
1 ripe avocado, peeled and sliced
4 whole canned green chilies, seeded and
    opened flat
Alfalfa sprouts
4 crusty hard rolls, split

1 Shape beef into 4 patties. Broil, pan fry, or grill to desired doneness. Season with salt and pepper to taste.

2 Top each patty with a cheese slice. Cover and continue to cook until cheese melts, about 2 minutes.

3 Place burger on roll and top with remaining ingredients.

Yield: 4 servings

Grilled Corleone

As Clemenza told Michael in *The Godfather,* you never know when you may have to cook for 20 or 30 guys holed up during a gang war. This delightful grilled Provolone sandwich—fragrant with basil and thick with tomato slices—would satisfy even Mama Corleone. It sings of Sicily from Lake Tahoe to Havana and is particularly apt as a pick-me-up during Senate hearings. This snack is an offering you can't refuse.

Preparation time: 6 minutes

> 2 slices pumpernickel bread
> 2 slices Provolone cheese
> 3 slices plum tomato
> 1 tsp chopped fresh basil
> Unsalted butter

1 Assemble sandwich by placing cheese and tomato on 1 bread slice. Sprinkle with basil and top with remaining bread slice.

2 Spread the outer sides of the sandwich with butter. Grill in a preheated frying pan until bread is toasted and cheese begins to melt. Turn and grill other side.

Yield: 1 sandwich

Stuffed Couch Potatoes

Using the VCR to its best advantage allows you to fix filling foods rather than simple snacks. These twice-baked potatoes fit the bill nicely. They are hot and tasty, almost a meal by themselves. Like all good Couch Potato food, these potatoes have a variety of fillings that can be tailored to fit the mood of the movie you are watching.

Basic Baked Potato

The foundation of all good Stuffed Couch Potatoes is the Basic Baked Potato.

**Preparation time: microwave oven—10 minutes
conventional oven—50 minutes**

1 Preheat conventional oven to 425°.
2 Scrub 1 medium baking potato and prick with a fork.
3 Microwave potato on high, 5 to 6 minutes, until tender. In a conventional oven, bake potato at 425° about 45 minutes.
4 Split baked potato.
5 Top with one of the following toppings.

Thin Man Spud

Nick and Nora Charles were generally too busy solving crimes to finish a meal (or a drink). Even when they had the time, they would never think of eating a potato dressed merely with butter, though this sour cream and caviar creation would do nicely. There's no use begging for leftovers, Asta darling, there are none.

Preparation time: 10 minutes

*½ cup sour cream
1 tsp chopped chives
1 large baking potato
1 tb butter
2 ozs whitefish caviar*

1 In a small bowl combine sour cream and chives. Set aside.
2 Cut potato into 8 slices.
3 Melt butter in skillet over medium heat. Sauté

potato 3 minutes per side. Drain on paper towel.

4 Top each potato slice with a generous dollop of the sour cream mixture and garnish with a teaspoon of caviar. Serve warm.

Yield: 8 servings

Sierra Madre Potato

Controversy rages about the cause of Bogart's murderous behavior in *The Treasure of the Sierra Madre*. Was it lust for gold? Sadism? Paranoia? The answer may have been hunger. Since the gold mine lacked an oven, there was no way for the prospectors to bake these potatoes heaped with chili and Monterey Jack. You the viewer are more fortunate. You can even toss in a jalapeño pepper in case any banditos ride over the couch.

Preparation time: microwave oven—3 minutes
conventional oven—20 minutes

1 baked potato
¼ cup prepared chili
1 tb chopped onion
2 tbs shredded Monterey Jack cheese
1 sliced jalapeño pepper (if you dare!)
Sour cream
Shredded lettuce
1 tomato, diced

1 Stuff baked potato with chili, onion, cheese, and pepper.

2 Microwave on high 30 to 45 seconds. In a conventional oven, preheat to 400°. Bake potato for 15 minutes or until cheese melts.

3 Garnish with sour cream, shredded lettuce, and diced tomato if desired.

Yield: 1 serving

Road to Idaho
Potato

1 baked potato
1 oz diced ham
1 tb sliced green onion
2 tbs shredded, sharp Cheddar cheese

This recipe pays homage to the biggest Ham and Cheese of their day—Bob Hope and Bing Crosby. It was originally designed to be used in what was to have been the first U.S.-based "Road" picture, *The Road to Idaho,* but it's just as fitting for the duo's trips to Zanzibar or Bali.

Preparation time: microwave oven—3 minutes
conventional oven—20 minutes

1 Fill baked potato with ham, onion, and cheese.
2 Microwave on high for 30 seconds or until cheese melts. In a conventional oven, preheat to 425° and bake for 15 minutes.
Yield: 1 serving

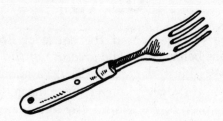

FRINGE FOODS FOR FRINGE VIEWING

Some television shows are so inventive that they defy categorization. They don't fit the usual structure or audience, so they must make a path for themselves. These are the programs we celebrate in "Fringe Viewing."

Most of the programming in this section differs from prime-time and late-night programming because of its odd time slot, irregular running time, or unusual purpose. MTV is a classic example. Playing only music videos around the clock, MTV makes no attempt to achieve balance with newscasts or variety hours. MTV's success, and that of other strange single-note offspring (the Health Channel, the Home Shopping Club) demonstrate the adaptability of this concept and the single-mindedness of some Spuds.

Other programming qualifies for fringe viewing simply because it cannot be understood by the majority of the viewing audience. A prime example of this type of show is the Spanish *novela,* or soap opera. Its soliloquies and rapid-fire exchanges may be unintelligible to English-speaking viewers, but its histrionics put "Dallas" and "Falcon Crest" to shame.

Then there is "Pee Wee's Playhouse." This show does not defy any of the constructs of regular programming: it is in English, it airs in a reasonable Saturday morning time slot, and runs for a mere 30 minutes. Yet, somehow, it eludes all convention and, for that reason, must be listed here.

To celebrate these various types of fringe programs, we've developed a group of equally varied "Fringe Foods." These foods capture the idiosyncrasies of the palate as resoundingly as these shows tackle the oddities of viewing taste. Accordingly, we top off this section with a tribute to the Original Fringe Food, the Twinkie.

"Bodywatch" Spread

After "Red" Duke explains the dire consequences of high cholesterol levels in laboratory rats and rides his palomino into the sunset, prepare this ricotta spread. You can feel healthy and righteous eating it with sliced vegetables and low-salt crackers.

Preparation time: 7 minutes

1 15-oz container skim-milk ricotta
1 tsp dried basil
½ tsp lemon-pepper seasoning
1 small clove garlic, minced
Salt to taste
1 tb olive oil
Assorted fresh vegetables for dipping,
  sliced
Garlic melba toast

1 Place ricotta in a sieve and let all liquid drain while assembling remaining ingredients.

2 In a bowl, combine drained ricotta and seasonings. Form into a mound at the center of a serving platter. Drizzle spread with olive oil.

3 Arrange vegetables and melba toast around spread.

Yield: 2 cups

MTV Munch

Even more than you want your MTV, you want something to munch. This snack unites a number of old standards with a new cover.

Preparation time: 5 minutes
Baking time: 15 minutes

3 qts unsalted popcorn, popped
1 10-oz package slim pretzel sticks
2 cups dry roasted peanuts
½ cup butter, melted
1 tsp garlic powder
1 tsp seasoned salt
1 tsp Worcestershire sauce

1 Preheat oven to 250°.

2 In a large baking or roasting pan, mix popped popcorn, pretzels, and peanuts.

3 In a separate bowl, combine remaining ingredients, and pour over popcorn mixture. Toss to coat with butter.

4 Bake for 15 minutes. Stir several times while heating.

Yield: 5 quarts

Dip *Dolorosa*

You don't have to be Spanish to love Spanish soap operas. Granted, these hour-long segments of romance and mayhem are especially addictive for Spanish-speaking housewives, who watch them faithfully, weeping with the heroines and booing the villains. Titles like *"Mi Amada* (My Beloved) *Beatriz"* and *"Los Ricos También Lloran"* ("The Rich Also Cry") proclaim the novela's twin concerns of love and sorrow. But more and more gringo Potatoes, pausing in their restless search through the UHF channels, find they enjoy these novelas. Some of the dialogue may even be improved for not being understood.

In keeping with the characters' troubles, this dip has been christened "Sorrowful," but you'll find this blend of cheese and chilies as pleasing as the novelas' happy endings.

Preparation time: 8 minutes

> *1 16-oz package Cheddar cheese, cubed*
> *1 cup milk*
> *1 4-oz can chopped green chilies*
> *2 tbs flour*

1 In a food processor or blender, process all ingredients on high until smooth.

2 Pour into a saucepan or fondue pot. Cook and stir over a low heat until thickened, about 6 minutes.

3 Serve with corn chips or cubes of French bread.

Yield: 3½ cups

Jack LaLanne Fruit Kebobs

Jack LaLanne is the godfather of the exercise program—he was telling you how to tone those thighs long before Jane Fonda discovered leg warmers. While watching one of his aerobic workouts, you can eat this treat with a clear conscience.

Preparation time: 3 minutes

> 3 cups mixed fresh fruit chunks (melon,
> strawberries, grapes, apples, mangoes)
> 1 tb lime juice
> 1 8-oz carton plain yogurt
> 1 tb honey

1 Sprinkle fruit with lime juice.
2 Thread fruit pieces on wooden skewers.
3 Combine yogurt with juices left in the bowl and drizzle yogurt sauce over kebobs. Serve immediately.

Yield: 4 servings

A Salute to Pee Wee Herman

Some people like Pee Wee Herman for his voice, his wardrobe, or his dancing abilities. Couch Potatoes love him for his culinary prowess.

Pee Wee Herman is the Julia Child of the Saturday morning set. He prepares so many recipes on "Pee Wee's Playhouse" that he could turn the Playhouse into a cooking school. Pee Wee knows the elements of Couch Potato cooking—ease and quantity—and demonstrates them with panache and enthusiasm. His ice cream soup is a classic of simplicity.

So you can share in the cooking fun, we offer two Pee Wee specials, created in our kitchens, but inspired by the master chef himself. Prepare them early in the morning and share them with the entire Playhouse gang.

Pee Wee's Caramel Apples

These colorful treats will be perfect for Pee Wee's fall harvest party, as long as all the ingredients aren't eaten during the bobbing for apples contest earlier in the day.

Preparation time: microwave oven—9 minutes
conventional stove—15 minutes

1 14-oz package caramels
2 tbs hot water
6 firm tart apples
6 wooden sticks
¾ cup candy-coated chocolate candies
¾ cup bittersweet chocolate bits
¾ cup roasted cashew bits
¾ cup sprinkles

1 Unwrap caramels while watching TV.

2 Place unwrapped caramels in a buttered, deep, microwave glass bowl. Add water, cover, and microwave on high 3 minutes or until melted. Stir twice during heating. For conventional stove, place caramels and water in a double boiler. Melt over medium-low heat.

3 While the caramels are melting, insert a wooden stick in the stem end of each apple. Dip into melted caramel mixture, turning apple until well coated.

4 Dip apple bottoms immediately into favorite crunchy coatings and place on wax paper. Place in freezer for 5 minutes, until cool.

Yield: 6 servings

Pee Wee's Cheesy Onion Puffs

If the Playhouse gang hosts a cocktail party, these morsels will be essential to Pee Wee's instruction on the Art of Canapé Eating. Pink ginger ale in plastic champagne glasses is the necessary accompaniment.

Preparation time: 2 minutes
Baking time: 10 minutes

> *1 cup mayonnaise*
> *½ cup grated Parmesan cheese*
> *1 tb dried onion flakes*
> *30 snack rye or pumpernickel bread slices*

1 Preheat oven to 425°.
2 Combine mayonnaise, cheese, and onion.
3 Spread 1 tablespoon mayonnaise mixture on each bread slice.
4 Bake for 10 minutes until puffs are golden.
Yield: 30 snacks

Homage to the Twinkie™: The Perfect Sick-Day Snack

Some foods may be sweeter, some brighter, some puffier. But it's hard to beat these orange-colored, cream-filled shortcakes for sheer stolen pleasure. You wouldn't dare snack on them during staff meetings or pull one out at a business lunch. Health-conscious friends might gasp; even Mom worried they'd rot your teeth. Twinkies are strictly for those times when it's you, the couch, and the TV.

Like signatures and neuroses, Twinkie-eating patterns are established in childhood and persist in later life. Those of us who didn't get them in our lunch boxes enjoyed them as after-school snacks. We associated them with syndicated and rerun cartoons. Rocky the Flying Squirrel, Gigantor the Robot, and Underdog soared high over our Twinkies. George of the Jungle may have stashed them in his vines. The Jetsons kept them in their push-button kitchen. Every cartoon character, from the rubbery Popeye of Max

Fleischer to the stiff Japanese Speed Racer, oversaw our spongy meal.

One of the disadvantages of adulthood is that most workplaces make room for neither cartoons nor Twinkies. The only solution is the time-honored childhood one of calling in sick. (Not needing your mother to make the call is one of the few advantages of adulthood.) Once again, you can sit in guilty but contented abandon, wrapped in blankets, shielded from the afternoon by a box of Twinkies and a slew of cartoons. "Diver Dan" and "Crusader Rabbit" may be no more. You may have to settle for limited 1980s animation of jerky lip motions and angular punches. But though the cartoon may be wooden, the Twinkie bounces on.

SEMPER TWINKIE

Pinkie Twinkie™ Shortcake

Who says natural foods and Twinkies don't mix? Twinkies' colors match everything. If strawberries aren't available, try a Peachy Twinkie Shortcake with peaches or a Twinkieberry Shortcake with blueberries. Eat them while watching Technicolor™ Looney Tunes.

Preparation time: 45 seconds

> *1 8-oz package frozen strawberries in syrup, defrosted*
> *2 packages Twinkies*

1 Split each Twinkie down the center lengthwise.
2 Top each Twinkie with ¼ cup sliced strawberries with syrup.
Yield: 2 to 4 servings

Twinkie™ Splits

Inspired by Double Stuf and Big Stuf Oreos, this all-white sundae is for anyone who has ever lamented that Twinkies don't have enough cream. The varieties of sugar—the marshmallow cream, vanilla ice cream, and whipped cream—speed up your system when slow animation drags you down.

Preparation time: 5 minutes

> *3 scoops vanilla ice cream*
> *1 Twinkie, split*
> *3 tbs marshmallow cream*
> *Whipped cream to taste*

1 Place ice cream in long, boat-shaped bowl. Buttress with Twinkie, as with bananas in banana splits.
2 Spoon marshmallow cream over ice cream and top with whipped cream.

Yield: 1 serving

Lunch with the Home Shopping Club: When the Couch Potato Wants to Make a Deal

Going to the mall used to be fun—until you became a member of the Couch Potato family. Now it takes you away from the television set. That's why the Home Shopping Club is a blessing. It allows you to do all the things you like to do at the mall in the privacy of your own couch. You can experience the flash of pleasure that comes from buying a bargain, engage in intimate banter with the salespeople, *and* you can watch TV to boot.

With this special Home Shopping Club Lunch, you can also eat to your heart's content. These recipes are designed to honor the things that make the HSC a joy—they are as happy as the voices of the sales consultants and as satisfying as the bargains. The Shopping Club Sandwich is just like the club itself: it brings together a wide variety of ingredients under one roof. To accompany it, try the happiest drink ever invented—the Perky Pink Lemonade, made with ever-effervescent sparkling water. (We developed it to pay homage to the round-the-clock sales announcers, who are unmatched in their optimism and perseverance.) To end your snack, we've created the Jeweled Cubes, which are as golden as a 14-carat herringbone chain and as colorful as an emerald, ruby, and cubic zirconia ring.

As if these culinary enticements themselves aren't enough, these recipes also fit into your shopping and viewing schedule. With the HSC Lunch, you won't miss one minute of bargain-hunting!

Perky Pink Lemonade

The truly amazing thing about the Home Shopping Club is not the assortment of merchandise, but how the salespeople manage to stay so cheerful and bub-bly throughout their shift. Surely they never drink anything stronger than our Perky Pink Lemonade.

Preparation time: 10 minutes

1½ cups lemon juice (6 lemons)
¾ cup sugar
5 cups seltzer water
3 drops red food coloring
Maraschino cherries

1 Juice and strain lemons. Pour into pitcher.
2 Add water, sugar, and food coloring, stir until sugar is blended and color is an even pink.
3 Pour over ice in tall glasses and garnish with cherries.
Yield: 6 servings

Shopping Club Sandwich

Just as each few minutes of the Home Shopping Club brings new surprises, each level of the Shopping Club Sandwich yields new taste treats. There are two kinds of luncheon meats, two cheeses, and two breads. It also serves the home shopper's most crucial food need: on-phone eatability. When you've just started your sandwich and a must-have bargain shows up on screen, hold the sandwich in one hand and dial with the other.

Preparation time: 12 minutes

8 slices white bread, crusts trimmed
4 slices whole wheat bread, crust trimmed
Mayonnaise
Iceberg lettuce
8 slices Colby Cheddar cheese
12 slices turkey breast
12 slices Virginia baked ham
8 slices Swiss cheese

1 Arrange bread in 3 rows of 4 slices each, with the middle row the wheat bread.
2 Spread all tops with mayonnaise.
3 On row of bread closest to you, place lettuce, Colby cheese, and turkey.
4 Top with whole wheat bread.
5 Add more lettuce and ham and Swiss cheese.
6 Top with white bread, mayonnaise side down.
7 Slice in diagonals and pierce with cocktail toothpicks, if desired.

Yield: 4 servings

Jeweled Cubes

When the time runs out before you place your order for the cubic zirconia ruby and emerald ring, console yourself with these lemony bars that sparkle with a jellybean topping crafted in your favorite zirconia colors. And keep watching—as soon as they've featured the radar detector and porcelain clown doll, they'll come back with an even better zirconia bargain.

Preparation time: 10 minutes
Chilling time: 60 minutes

1 cup graham cracker crumbs
5 tbs butter
⅓ cup granulated sugar
8-oz package cream cheese
2 tbs lemon juice
½ cup confectioners' sugar
12-oz bag jellybeans

1 Preheat oven to 425°.
2 To make crust, melt butter in 8-inch square oven-proof pan. Mix graham cracker crumbs and granulated sugar together.
3 Add crumbs and sugar to melted butter and blend thoroughly. Press mixture evenly over bottom of pan with spoon.
4 Bake crust for 7 minutes.
5 While crust is baking, mix together cream cheese, lemon, and confectioners' sugar.
6 Take crust out of oven and pour in cream cheese mixture. Chill for 1 hour.
7 Just before serving, top with layer of jellybeans. Make sure to remove all the black ones first.

Yield: 9 servings

THE COUCH POTATO PARTY PLANNER:

THE COCKTAIL PARTY OF THE '80S

Contrary to popular opinion, the cocktail party is not dead. It has merely evolved to a (dare we say?) higher form: the Couch Potato party. The benefits of the Couch Potato party over the cocktail party are many. You don't have to asphyxiate yourself with silk ties or torture your feet with spike heels. You are no longer expected to engage in excruciatingly banal small talk or deliver a barrage of *bon mots* (Couch Potatoes prefer bonbons). You don't have to stand around trying to balance a martini glass and a skewer of Swedish meatballs without staining your shirt. At a Couch Potato party, the keynote is comfort: you can wear comfortable clothes, use paper plates, and still enjoy your evening's viewing.

The purpose of a Couch Potato party is simple: to bring together groups larger than your immediate family to watch a particular event on TV and to eat. There are two specific types of events that demand group participation:

1. *Events that you need moral support to watch*, such as season openers.

2. *Events that you naturally watch in a group*, for example, sports championships and holiday movies, such as *It's a Wonderful Life*.

In this more relaxed age, many former social barriers have been lifted. You are no longer required to dress for dinner, leave calling cards, or be ashamed to watch shows that are "not our kind." But informality does not mean sacrificing graciousness. A successful Couch Potato party requires more than great quantities of food and a large screen.

First and foremost, a Couch Potato party requires a theme, a reason for your fellow Tubers to venture forth from their dens and familiar couches to come to your gathering. It is not enough to say, "I need moral support while watching the new fall lineup because they may have killed off my favorite character." Instead, send an invitation that says, "Couch Potato Party to Welcome Back Your Favorite Thursday Night Friends."

Now that your Couch Potato party has a theme, you need to prepare food that supports it. The parties outlined in the Party Planner are but a starting point for your themes and matching menus; with a little imagination, the *TV Guide* is the limit.

Most of the recipes in this book are timed to specific breaks in programming. These menus are different. As your mother told you many times, a successful party depends on good *planning*. That means preparing ahead: most of these recipes should be prepared *before* your guests arrive, so that you too can watch the event you're celebrating.

It is also important to make sure your guests are aware of proper Couch Potato etiquette. The rules are few but essential. They are meant to ensure that everyone can fully enjoy both elements of a Couch Potato party: the eating and the viewing.

Couch Potato Party Rules

1 The host should arrange the cushions and couches so everyone has a clear view of the television set.
2 The host should make sure that all food is conveniently located.
3 Guests should refrain from throwing objects at the television, with the exception of popcorn.
4 Guests should refrain from standing in front of the television screen.
5 To prevent brawls, the host should retain possession of the remote control.

Couch Potatoes unite! You have nothing to lose but your solitude!

THE WIDE WORLD OF SPORTS PARTIES

Historically, watching sports occupies an important place in the evolution of the Couch Potato lifestyle. Formerly, sports watching could be done only outside the home with hordes of strangers, eating from the limited menus provided by stadiums. With the advent of television, however, the advantages of watching games from the comfort of the home became immediately obvious. There were no hassles with traffic or parking, and no anxiety about getting enough tickets or a good seat for the big game. The first recorded incident of eating while watching TV occurred on September 30, 1947, during the opening-day broadcast of the Yankee–Dodgers World Series. Mr. Walter Herlocker, of Queens, was overcome during the top of the third inning by a desire for a hot dog and beer, which inspired him to venture into the kitchen during a conference on the pitcher's mound. This first crude attempt at Couch Potato style resulted in Mr. Herlocker missing the crucial third out, but discovering the pleasures of eating as many hot dogs as he wanted without waiting for the vendor to return.

Thus the groundwork for Couch Potato life was laid—extended viewing was happily paired with eating.

Sports watching, true to its robust outdoor roots, still holds special hazards. It frequently inspires behavior not often observed in other Couch Potato activities: sudden frantic movement. Under the influence of passionate moments such as a final-second slam dunk in overtime in the NBA Playoffs, Couch Potatoes have been known to rise from their sofas, flailing their arms, and shouting, even springing into the air. Bad calls from referees have provoked outbursts of throwing food at the TV screen and abuse of innocent nearby cats. Obviously, this impulsive behavior can be dangerous, leading to stained couches, fugitive food under the coffee table, and interrupted viewing. There have been cases of more serious damage, including remote controls rendered useless from being crushed by a careless leap from the couch and more dreadful still, screens shorted out from being pelted by half-full beer cans.

To avoid such mishaps, COCOPUFS (the Council of Couch Potatoes United for Food Safety) has drawn up the following rules for sports watching:

1. Always place food and drinks on a TV tray or coffee table during viewing. Recommended distance from the couch is 18 inches. Anything closer can be toppled during sudden movement.
2. Avoid serving foods that stick on impact to TV screen or floor.
3. Never place the remote control on the floor during a game.
4. Always watch with a friend. Other watchers may increase the chances for spills and stains, but can prevent more serious accidents, such as battered TVs or other property damage.

To aid fans in abiding by Rule #4, we have developed several party menus tailored for sports watching. The Super Bowl Party is already an established tradition for many Couch Potatoes, and we offer a menu that moves beyond the classic beer-and-chips fare associated with Super Sunday. The World Series Marathon Party includes all the ballpark ritual food so dear to the fan's heart. (Baseball fans are a superstitious lot and would not risk jinxing their team by watching while eating unorthodox food.) For tennis fans, our Breakfast at Wimbledon is light but satisfying, just the thing for celebrating those smashing serves, lightning volleys, and the pristine symmetry of the sunlit court. If you like the basics, no silly sticks or balls, just man-to-man, winner take all, then the Bunkhouse Bash is for you. With friends and the right food, watching any sport can be a party.

Super Bowl Party

Just as watching sports on television inspired the beginning of the Couch Potato lifestyle, the Super Bowl Party holds pride-of-place as the most widely celebrated of the Couch Potato parties. It began in the early 1970s, when tales of "football widows" began to circulate. These women were neglected by their husbands for major portions of weekends during football season. Their worst day was Super Bowl Sunday, when TV sets across America were tuned to the big event and other family members were warned, under threat of bodily harm, not to disturb the impassioned watcher. Historians speculate that the first Super Bowl parties were organized by football widows in an attempt to confine the damage to a minimum number of houses in the neighborhood. Fans also discovered the advantages of having friends present so that all bets could be settled while last-minute instant replays were shown.

Although there are female football fans, the Super Bowl Party is still primarily a male-bonding event, which calls for hearty, two-fisted foods. Our menu selections may seem a bit messy, but that's part of the fun—Super Sloppy Joes are not meant to be eaten with crooked pinkies. The spicy Macho Nachos will soon have the gang roaring for more. Don't worry, you can hold them at the five-yard line (or at least the kitchen door) with our Two Minute Time-Out Dip. During halftime you can combat the boredom of watching yet another silly band marching to the theme from *Rocky* with our Chocolate Astroturf Cookies. Whether your team made it to the big game or not, your Super Bowl Party will be the star event of the winter viewing season.

Two Minute Time-Out Dip

When the coach has called a time-out and the team is huddling on the field, it's time for you to refill the chip bowl and whip up this quick onion dip.
Preparation time: 2 minutes

> *2 cups sour cream*
> *2 envelopes beef bouillon powder*
> *2 green onions, sliced*

1 Combine all ingredients in a bowl and stir well.
2 Serve immediately with chips or your favorite vegetable dippers.
Yield: 2¼ cups

Macho Nachos

These spicy nachos would warm up even those poor, scantily clad cheerleaders on the sidelines. Piled high with chilies, olives, and peppers, these nachos are not just a snack, they are almost a meal—so have a fork handy.

Preparation time: microwave oven—15 minutes
conventional oven—30 minutes

30 to 40 large, triangular tortilla chips
1 15½-oz can refried beans
1½ cups shredded Monterey Jack or
  Cheddar cheese
4 green onions, thinly sliced
¼ cup sliced, pitted black olives
Chopped green chilies or jalapeño
  peppers to taste
Sour cream
Guacamole (see page 15)

1 Spread each chip with 1 to 2 teaspoons refried beans. Arrange on a large oven-proof or microwave-safe platter.

2 Top chips with cheese, onion, olives, and chilies or peppers.

3 Microwave on medium-high 1½ to 3 minutes or until cheese has melted. In a conventional oven, warm nachos at 400° for 10 to 15 minutes.

4 Serve with sour cream and/or guacamole.

Yield: 4 servings

Super Sloppy Joes

These man-sized sandwiches are beefy, zesty, and hot. We suggest you take bites during the instant replays because sudden movements inspired by a successful 50-yard pass while holding this sandwich could have unfortunate results for your immediate environment.
Preparation time: 20 to 30 minutes

1 tb butter or margarine
1 lb lean ground beef
1 medium onion, chopped
½ cup chopped celery
½ cup chopped green pepper
1 cup barbecue sauce
1 tsp prepared mustard
6 to 8 hamburger buns, split

1 In a skillet, melt butter over medium heat. Cook ground beef and vegetables until meat is browned. Drain any excess fat.

2 Add barbecue sauce and mustard. Simmer, covered, for 15 to 20 minutes.

3 Keep mixture warm until halftime. Serve on hamburger buns.

Yield: 6 to 8 servings

Chocolate Astroturf Cookies

It's the fourth quarter, five minutes left, and the game is tied. Your team is conferring on the turf and you want to feel you're in there with them. Huddle in spirit with these lumpy, bumpy, fudgy oat treats. They may look like brown Astroturf, but the similarity ends there. They're actually one of the most addictive treats we know: you'll find yourself yelling for a time-out to rush to the kitchen for more.

Preparation time: 20 minutes
Chilling time: 30 minutes

1½ cups sugar
¼ cup cocoa
½ cup milk
½ cup butter
1 tsp vanilla
⅓ cup smooth peanut butter
⅔ cup chopped walnuts
3 cups quick-cooking oatmeal

1 Place sugar, cocoa, milk, and butter in large saucepan and cook over low heat for 4 minutes, stirring often. Do not bring to boil.

2 Add vanilla and peanut butter. Fold in oats and nuts.

3 Remove from heat and drop in rounded teaspoonfuls onto ungreased cookie sheets.

4 Chill in freezer for 30 minutes. Store in refrigerator.

Yield: 3 to 4 dozen cookies

Breakfast at Wimbledon

Now that the uncouth likes of Jimmy Connors and John McEnroe no longer dominate the courts, decorum is returning to tennis. The players accept their victories and defeats with courtesy and grace. The fans do not abuse the officials and make rude noises to break the concentration of the players. Obviously, watching tennis on TV calls for a menu that reflects this spirit.

Suitable for the occasion, our Breakfast at Wimbledon features quiet food. There are no breadsticks or chips to cause loud crunches and make it difficult to hear the soft-spoken commentators. The light, airy Wimbledon Omelet will cause only the gentle tinkle of knife and fork against china. The Hush Honey Muffins are distracting only when the last one is eaten. When a serve goes wild, calm yourself with a cool Rum Lob. Celebrate the finish with the Love Fruit Cup of strawberries topped with sour cream and honey. With a repast like this, you will always have plenty of takers when you ask, "Tennis breakfast, anyone?"

Rum Lob

When a famous British tennis player lost an important match at Wimbledon, the Cockney bartender at his favorite pub created this drink to take the sting out of his bad serve at the end of the set. The proper toast when drinking it is, "Rum Lobs to all yer foes."

Preparation time: 3 minutes

> 1 15¼-oz can crushed pineapple in its
>   own juice
> 3 cups vanilla ice cream
> ¾ cup light rum

1 Place all ingredients in a blender container.
2 Cover and process on high until smooth. Serve immediately.
Yield: 6 7-oz servings

Love Fruit Cup

Only a sport as refined as tennis would announce a score as "15–Love." When your favored hopeful has an off day, console yourself with our Love Fruit Cup, a simple yet elegant offering of strawberries and sour cream.

Preparation time: 4 minutes

>	*2 pints fresh strawberries, hulled*
>	*½ cup sour cream*
>	*4 tsps honey*

1 Divide strawberries evenly between 4 dessert cups or small bowls.

2 In a separate bowl, mix sour cream and honey until well blended.

3 Top strawberries with cream mixture, about 2 tablespoons each. Can be chilled before serving.

Yield: 4 servings

Hush Honey Muffins

Once the match has begun, feast on these fluffy muffins. They have no noisy nuts to cause distracting crunching during a serve, nor any fussy extra ingredients to detract from the flavor of the butter and jam.

Preparation time: 15 minutes
Baking time: 20 to 25 minutes

>	*1 egg*
>	*1 cup milk*
>	*¼ cup corn oil*
>	*¼ cup honey*
>	*3 tsps baking powder*
>	*2 cups whole wheat flour*
>	*1 tsp salt*

1 Preheat oven to 400°.
2 Grease a 12-cup muffin tin.
3 Combine egg, milk, oil, honey, and baking powder.
4 Stir in salt and flour until flour is just moistened.
5 Pour into muffin tin, filling cups within ½ inch of rim.
6 Bake for 20 to 25 minutes or until golden brown.
7 Remove from tin immediately and serve.
Yield: 12 muffins

Wimbledon Omelet

Prepare this omelet after the Hush Honey Muffins are in the oven. It is so quick that you can whip up two or three while the announcers are still whispering about the history of Ivan Lendl's punishing forehand serves. Sour cream, chives, and sharp Cheshire cheese give the omelet an English flavor in honor of the location.

Preparation time: 10 minutes

4 eggs
¼ cup sour cream
½ tsp salt
1 tsp snipped chives
1½ tbs butter
¼ cup grated Cheshire cheese

1 In a bowl, whip together eggs, sour cream, salt, and chives.
2 Melt butter in omelet pan. Have the serving plate near by.
3 When butter is sizzling, but not burning, add egg mixture. As the edges begin to set, with one hand lift the handle of the pan. As the eggs run to the bottom side, lift the edge of the omelet to let the uncooked eggs run underneath. Tip the pan the other way and repeat the process.
4 When the omelet is cooked, but not burned, add cheese to the side away from the handle. Tip the pan up, fold the handle side over the filling, and then flip the whole omelet onto the plate.
Yield: 2 servings

World Series Marathon

The first World Series party was celebrated in 1947 and immediately became a Couch Potato institution. Now entering their fourth decade of existence, these seven-day extravaganzas have survived five commissioners of baseball, the electronic scoreboard, and the coming of Astroturf.

A World Series Marathon begins with the first strains of the opening-day "Star-Spangled Banner" and ends with the final Series wrap-up. Its plan is simple: to re-create, in the comfort of your home, the time-honored chaos of a championship series. This includes the scorecards, the banners, the car window dolls with the bobbing heads, and the *food*.

In creating this World Series menu, we followed a simple, Berra-like rule: "If it ain't broke, don't fix it." Rather than create baseball-shaped sushi or tofu fries, we stuck to the basics—gigantic hot dogs, chewy, gooey caramel corn, and tart lemonade. Our Triple Play Hot Dogs, with their hearty beer-and-sauerkraut filling, satisfy like a game-winning home run in the bottom of the ninth. The scrumptious Peanut-Caramel Corn is as choice as a 3–0 lead with tonight's game at home. The Old-Fashioned Lemonade is simple and perfect, like a cleanly executed double play that ends the final game. Pair these selections with some beer and hard pretzels, and you'll be set until the locker-room champagne toast.

Old-Fashioned Lemonade

Before there was Gatorade, there was lemonade. This classic thirst quencher is nearly as old as baseball itself; its anniversary predates the last Cubs World Series and Joe Garagiola's first television baseball commentary. In this modern version of the recipe, we've cut down on the sugar to give the lemonade a tangy twist that befits the more frequent brawls of today's game.

Preparation time: 8 minutes

> 1 cup lemon juice (4 lemons)
> 3 cups water
> ⅓ cup sugar
> 2 tbs honey

1 Juice and strain lemons. Pour into pitcher.
2 Add water, sugar, and honey. Stir until honey dissolves.
3 Pour over ice in tall glass.

Yield: 4 servings

Triple Play Hot Dogs

Like an inning with a perfect bunt, a home run, and a stolen base, Triple Play Hot Dogs unite three classic baseball elements: hot dogs, sauerkraut, and beer. May these and your team be always on a roll.

Preparation time: 35 minutes

> 6 old-fashioned hot dogs (with skins)
> 1 8-oz can sauerkraut, drained
> 1 cup beer
> 1 tsp caraway seeds
> 6 French-style hard rolls
> Spicy mustard

1 In a Dutch oven or saucepan combine franks, sauerkraut, beer, and caraway seeds. Cover and bring to a boil.
2 Reduce heat to simmer and cook 30 minutes.
3 Drain and serve frankfurters on a crusty roll. Top with sauerkraut.

Yield: 6 servings

Peanut-Caramel Corn

Hot dogs may provide the long-term protein to get you through the game, but chewy caramel corn gives you the pickup you need to survive those tense, slow-moving middle innings. When munched with the proper intensity, it also makes enough noise to drown out unacceptable announcer commentary. This Peanut-Caramel Corn is not for the faint of teeth.
Preparation time: 30 minutes

¾ cup roasted peanuts
⅔ cup popcorn kernels
1 cup light brown sugar, firmly packed
6 tbs butter
¼ cup light corn syrup
½ cup water
½ tsp vanilla

1 Preheat oven to 275°.
2 Place peanuts on 7″ × 9″ jelly roll pan and bake for 10 minutes. Turn off oven but keep peanuts inside to remain warm.
3 Pop popcorn while peanuts are roasting. Put popped popcorn and peanuts in large stainless-steel bowl, and place in oven.
4 In a deep pot (to avoid splattering), heat brown sugar, butter, corn syrup, and water, stirring often, until mixture reaches rolling boil.
5 Continue cooking sugar mixture, without stirring, until it reaches 260° to 265° on candy thermometer (hard crack stage), or until ½ teaspoon of mixture dropped in cold water forms solid but not brittle thread.
6 Immediately remove caramel from heat and add vanilla.
7 Drizzle peanut mixture with caramel sauce, and mix thoroughly. Let dry on cookie sheet. Break apart if necessary.
Yield: 3 quarts

Bunkhouse Bash

In spite of the circus atmosphere of most matches, wrestling fans have simple tastes. There are good guys and bad guys, winners and losers, and everybody knows who is who. Fans love the drama, the mascots, flashy costumes, and outrageous boasting, but they know that it is just a way of psyching everyone up for the main event. When the bell rings, Jake the Snake puts his boa back in the bag, Brutus Beefcake puts down his barber shears, the Honky Tonk Man puts down his guitar, and the fight begins. When all the bragging and playacting is over, it still comes down to just two wrestlers in the ring, each using his strength and skill to defeat his opponent. None of this nonsense about "I just want to do my best and better my own record." The goal may seem to be a title or to settle a grudge, but wrestlers are really only out for one thing: to beat the other guy.

Our Bunkhouse Bash features a menu as power-packed as the sport itself. The only drink that should be served at a wrestling party is a case or more of your favorite beer, so you have lots of cans to crush. The

Hulk Hoagie is as much of a crowd pleaser as its awesome namesake, the Hulkster himself. Provide an assortment of big bowls of chips for dipping in our fiery Hammerlock Dip, a brawny blend of horseradish and mustard. To celebrate the end of the bout and to cool down inflamed tempers, serve the Body Slam Sundae, a dessert guaranteed to keep you down for the count.

Hammerlock Dip

This powerful dip is not for the fainthearted. A macho blend of horseradish, garlic, and mustard, it could put hair on the chest of Ravishing Rick Rude and on the head of King Kong Bundy.

Preparation time: 1 minute

> 3 tbs horseradish
> 1 clove garlic, minced
> 1 tsp ground black pepper
> ½ cup sour cream
> ½ cup brown mustard

1 Combine all ingredients in a serving bowl and stir until well blended.

2 Chill until ready to serve with your favorite chips.

Yield: 1 cup

Hulk Hoagie

World Wrestling Federation champion Hulk Hogan is a 300-pound mighty slab of muscle and a wonder to behold inside the ring. He didn't get that way by eating milk toast. His mama probably fed him something like our Hulk Hoagie, a man-sized sandwich piled high with salami and cheese. It's enough to feed a crowd, unless your best friend is Andre the Giant.

Preparation time: 15 minutes

> 1 round, unsliced loaf of French or Italian bread, about 8 to 9 inches in diameter
> Softened butter or margarine
> 1 qt shredded lettuce
> ¼ cup mayonnaise
> 1 green pepper, sliced in rings
> 2 medium tomatoes, sliced
> ½ lb cotto salami, sliced
> ½ lb provolone cheese, sliced

1 Slice bread into 3 layers horizontally. Remove a little excess bread from each layer to make cutting easier.
2 Spread with softened butter.
3 Combine lettuce and mayonnaise. Spread on bottom layer. Top with green pepper and tomato slices.
4 Top with middle bread slice. Arrange salami and cheese on middle slice. Top with last piece of bread.
5 Cut into wedges to serve.
Yield: 6 to 8 servings

Body Slam Sundae

Only the most outraged and disappointed wrestling fan could refuse a Body Slam Sundae, with its mighty combination of ice cream, cookies, strawberries, and chocolate. Only a Tuber of great strength and willpower can overcome being pinned to the couch for the count of three after eating it.
Preparation time: 6 minutes

> *5 chocolate chip cookies*
> *3 scoops vanilla ice cream*
> *3 tbs strawberry preserves*
> *2 tbs chocolate syrup*

1 Seal cookies in a plastic bag and smash with an axhandle punch. Line bowl with crushed cookies.
2 Add 3 scoops of ice cream.
3 Top each scoop with strawberry preserves.
4 Drizzle chocolate syrup over everything and serve.
Yield: 1 serving

PROLONGED VIEWING

Couch POTATOES ®

SIC SEMPER POTATVM RECLINVS

CHIPS

SEASON OPENERS PARTY

The start of the new season is one of the most important occasions on the Couch Potato viewing agenda. It's a time to meet new friends and welcome back old ones. Familiar characters may have changed a bit, with new wardrobes (Sonny Crockett), more prominently receding hairlines (David Addison), or new physiques (Captain Kirk, who slimmed down for season openers, then chunked up for the winter). But it's also a time of anticipation and anxiety. You're still waiting for the resolution to your cliffhanger. (The terrorist-infested wedding on "Dynasty" nearly did you in a few years ago.) You're upset because two of your favorite shows have been scheduled in the same time slot, recalling the trauma of your youth when "Batman" came up against "Lost in Space." There's also the horror of discovering that a favorite show has been cancelled and banished to Programming Purgatory to wait for deliverance to Rerun

Heaven. The worst fate of all is when the cliffhangers are resolved in totally unsatisfactory fashion, as when an entire year of devotion to "Dallas" was dismissed as a bad dream or when Valerie was killed off in a fatal contract dispute and her family was left in the care of a skinny maiden aunt.

How do you survive these fears and frustrations? Unite your suffering fellow Couch Potatoes and throw a "Season Openers Party." This gathering of sympathetic souls is the closest a Tuber comes to having a support group. Only other Couch Potatoes can understand the terrors of the revelations of the new season. At the Season Openers Party, they can share their relief and their disappointment over the new programming.

The other consolation this party offers is the food. For our menu, we've combined all the qualities of a new season: the familiarity, the reliability, the surprises. Our Cop Show Crackers can be depended on to crunch on contact, like Spenser's fist in the face of a thug. The Sitcom Shrimp Dip blunts the sharp edges of your chips the way Larry, Darryl, and Darryl's bizarre pronouncements undercut Stephanie's self-absorption. The surprising combinations in our Mystery Chip Cookies are as gratifying as a string of Tracey Ullman skits. Soft drinks are the best thing to serve with these dishes: the bubbles will help keep your spirits up during a troubling hour of scheduling.

Fortified with friends and food, you can survive the slings and arrows of the new lineup with aplomb.

Sitcom Shrimp Dip

Sitcoms have been standard prime-time fare since the groundbreaking early days of "I Love Lucy." Whether your tastes run to "Married . . . with Children" or "Family Ties," this cool Sitcom Shrimp Dip will help the chips go down easy in between the laughs.

Preparation time: 8 minutes
Refrigeration time: 6 hours

11 ozs cream cheese (1 8-oz and
  1 3-oz package)
1 small onion, finely diced
1 clove garlic, minced
1 4½-oz can small shrimp, drained
  and chopped
1 dash Worcestershire sauce
1 dash hot red pepper sauce
6 tbs mayonnaise

1 Mix together first 6 ingredients until well blended. Refrigerate for several hours (at least 6) or overnight to allow the flavors to meld.

2 Bring to room temperature and fold in mayonnaise to a consistency satisfactory for scooping. Serve with chips.

Yield: Approximately 4 cups

Cop Show Crackers

While the seemingly unending appeal of cop shows is a mystery, the appeal of these crisp crackers is not. Savory with sesame seeds and cheese, they have a brisk taste that goes well with any of the variety of police shows airing almost every night.

Preparation time: 15 minutes
Shaping and baking time: 10 to 12 minutes

> 1 ¾ cups all-purpose flour
> ½ cup yellow cornmeal
> ½ tsp baking soda
> ½ tsp salt
> ½ cup butter
> 1½ cups shredded Cheddar cheese
> 2 tbs white vinegar
> ½ cup cold water
> ¼ cup sesame seeds

1 In a large mixing bowl, combine flour, cornmeal, baking soda, and salt.

2 Cut butter into flour mixture with a pastry blender or 2 knives, as you would for make pie pastry. Mixture will resemble a coarse meal.

3 Add cheese, vinegar, and cold water. Stir gently.

4 Shape into a ball and cover bowl. Chill 1 hour. The mixture will keep in the refrigerator up to 3 days.

5 When ready to serve, preheat oven to 375°. On a lightly floured board, roll ¼ of the dough into a 13-inch circle. Dough should be very thin.

6 Sprinkle with sesame seeds. Press seeds into dough with rolling pin. Cut into 8 wedges.

7 Place on greased cookie sheet. Bake 10 minutes or until crisp. Cool on a wire rack. Repeat with another section of dough if desired or save for later.

Yield: 32 crackers

Mystery Chip Cookies

Ever since Sam Malone proposed and David and Maddie got horizontal, the surprise has been gone from cliffhangers. This season, our delightful Mystery Chip Cookies will change all that. When your friends beg to know what's in these cookies, break into your sweetest Diane Chambers smile and say, "Wait until next time."

Preparation time: 10 minutes
Freezing time: 30 minutes
Baking time: 40 minutes

1 lb unsalted butter, cut into small chunks
1 cup sugar
1 tsp vanilla
1½ cups potato chips, crushed coarsely by hand
3½ cups flour
⅔ cups chopped walnuts or peanuts
½ cup confectioners' sugar (optional)

1 Preheat oven to 350°.
2 Cream butter, sugar, and vanilla until smooth.
3 Fold in potato chips, flour, and nuts.
4 Chill dough in freezer for at least 30 minutes.
5 Remove from freezer and form dough into 1¼-inch balls. Flatten each ball with a fork dipped in warm water.
6 Place on ungreased cookie sheet 1 inch apart and bake for 10 minutes.
7 Remove from oven and dust with confectioners' sugar, if desired.
Yield: 5 to 6 dozen cookies

POLITICAL PADDED PLATFORM PARTY

Once in a while, there are events in the real world that are covered extensively on TV, disrupting network schedules, and infringing on your TV quality time. These events, such as election night returns or State of the Union addresses, are usually highly unsettling and require the moral support of other Couch Potatoes to withstand.

Such times provide the perfect opportunity to throw a Political Padded Platform Party. Your friends will be just as frazzled as you, so what better solution than to gather together and eat? It will help all of you put everything into proper perspective.

With the right company and attitude, watching politicians can be as much fun as checking up on the "Lifestyles of the Rich and Famous." You may have watched many Presidential election nights, but not until you shared the event with others did you notice how those little multicolored maps of the U.S. employ Satanic color symbolism. Or that the idiosyncratic characters in Congressional hearings are remarkably similar to sitcom types: there's the defiant witness, special prosecutor, defense lawyer, tough Congressman, witty Congressman, and snoozing Congressman in the back row. Once you have learned how to view them, hearings are as addictive as soap operas. When you think of the political world in these terms, your petty annoyance becomes the theme for another Couch Potato party.

Invite your fellow Tubers over to your favorite padded platform for an evening of political theatre. The ever-helpful Couch Potato Party Planner has a menu of politically related (although perhaps not politically correct) food to start you on your way. Get your guests off their apathy with our feisty Strange Bedfellow Eggs, with their blend of sweet red and jalapeño peppers. Once they're on edge, cool them out with our Political Caper Salad, a smooth yet tangy mix of steak, capers, and vinaigrette. When the concession speeches start coming in, add to the sweetness and light with our fruity Election Cake. Finally, when the acceptance speeches begin, break out the Campaign Promises Champagne, a bubbly blend that is, appropriately, all fizz and no bite.

Political realities will never trouble you again.

Strange Bedfellow Eggs

Everyone at your party may be kindred spirits who voted for Pat Paulsen. But the political types on the screen will be the usual motley crew: candidates, aides, reporters, Secret Service agents, man-in-the-street interviewees in Podunk. These deviled eggs celebrate this diversity with a surprising pairing of peppers with an unexpected bite.

Preparation time: 20 minutes

> 6 eggs, hardcooked and peeled
> ¼ cup mayonnaise
> 1 tsp vinegar
> 1 tsp Dijon mustard
> 1 jalapeño pepper, chopped
> 1 tb sweet red pepper, finely chopped
> Dash garlic powder
> Dash cumin
> Salt and pepper to taste

1 Halve eggs lengthwise. Remove yolk and mash with mayonnaise, vinegar, and mustard. Fold in jalapeño pepper, red pepper, and seasonings.

2 Fill 12 egg whites with yolk mixture. Garnish with dash of chili pepper if desired.

Yield: 12 servings

Meaty Political Caper Salad

This salad is the perfect treat for watching Congressional hearings, when the bizarre thought patterns of people in government are exposed to public view. This unusual blending of tastes and textures will appeal to those who appreciate the irony of Watergate's "routine break-in" and Iranscam's "neat idea."

Preparation time: 15 minutes

2 tbs unsalted butter
2 lbs of beef tenderloin, cut into 1-inch
  chunks
¼ cup sour cream
¼ cup mayonnaise
1 tb capers
1 tb lemon juice
2 tsps Dijon mustard
Romaine leaves
2 medium tomatoes, sliced
2 green onions, thinly sliced

1 In a frying pan, melt butter on medium-high heat. Sauté meat until cooked to your preference. Remove from the heat.

2 Combine sour cream, mayonnaise, capers, lemon juice, and mustard. Toss with warm tenderloin.

3 Place on lettuce-lined platter or individual plates. Garnish with tomato slices and green onion. Serve with freshly ground black pepper. Serve immediately.

Yield: 6 servings

Campaign Promises Champagne

This bubbly drink is as sweet as a campaign promise. Like those heady vows, it hints at things it doesn't deliver and the bubbles burst very soon.

Preparation time: 2 minutes

⅔ cup sparkling white grape juice
⅓ cup seltzer

1 In a wine glass, pour sparkling grape juice and seltzer at the same time. Serve immediately before all the bubbles disappear.

Yield: 1 serving

Election Cake

When the results are in and the winning candidate is making his triumphant, but not too gloating, acceptance speech, it's time to break out the Election Cake. This is a variation of a traditional American recipe served in New England towns.

Preparation time: 20 minutes
Baking time: 30 to 35 minutes

2 cups all-purpose flour
1 tsp baking soda
1 tsp salt
½ cup shortening
1 cup sugar
2 eggs
½ cup sour cream
½ cup apple brandy
Rind of 1 orange
1 cup dried currants
1 cup chopped walnuts

GLAZE
Juice of 1 orange
2 tbs apple brandy
¼ cup sugar

1 Preheat oven to 350°.

2 Combine flour, baking soda, and salt. Set aside.

3 In a large mixing bowl, cream shortening and sugar until light and fluffy.

4 Add eggs, one at a time. Mix well. Add flour mixture alternately with sour cream and brandy until combined.

5 Fold in orange rind, currants, and chopped walnuts.

6 Pour into a greased 9″ × 13″ baking pan. Bake for 30 to 35 minutes.

7 When cake is removed from the oven, pour glaze over top of cake. Let cool.

8 Cake may be served with sweetened whipped cream or frosted with a basic butter-cream frosting.

Yield: 15 servings

THE *IT'S A WONDERFUL LIFE* PARTY

For some people, there are Christmas parties. For the true Couch Potato movie lover, there is only the *It's a Wonderful Life* Party.

It's a Wonderful Life has the distinction of becoming a national treasure by virtue of its being shown on television. When the film was released in 1946, it was not an unqualified success: it received mixed reviews and lost nearly half a million dollars. After that, the movie disappeared from sight, until 1974, when its copyright expired and was not extended, placing it in the public domain and available for free television holiday programming. This introduced the movie to a new generation. "I woke up one Christmas morning," director Frank Capra said, "and the whole world was watching *It's a Wonderful Life*." The first recorded *It's a Wonderful Life* Party was held in New York City in 1970, and celebrations across the country have been taking place ever since.

The *It's a Wonderful Life* Party usually takes place during the Christmas season, from Thanksgiving afternoon through Christmas evening, though with the magic of VCRs, it can happen anytime during the year when you need to be reminded that "No man is a failure who has friends."

We have focused our *It's a Wonderful Life* Party recipes on Clarence Odbody (Henry Travers), the Angel Second Class who earns his wings by showing George Bailey (James Stewart) what life would have been like if he had never been born. The festive Clarence's Flaming Rum Punch recalls one of the old-fashioned drinks the nearly 293-year-old Clarence requests when he and George visit Martini's Tavern. The ethereal, coconut-kissed Guardian Angel Cookies suggest a treat that George's wife Mary Bailey (Donna Reed) might have made to celebrate her husband's return to life.

These delectable recipes can be prepared in a very reasonable 90-minute to two-hour time span—less than the running time of a show you had intended to skip anyway, such as the colorized version of *It's a Wonderful Life.*

Other *It's a Wonderful Life* Party suggestions include:

• As guests enter, play "Buffalo Girls, Won't You Come Out Tonight?" on the Victrola;
• Get in the mood before the viewing by holding a Charleston Contest. Make sure that no pool exists beneath your dance floor;
• Have each guest bring a bell to mark the moment when Clarence gets his wings;
• If you want to show a double bill, follow *It's a Wonderful Life* with *The Bells of St. Mary's,* the movie playing at the Bedford Falls theater when George Bailey runs through town on Christmas Eve;
• Sing "Auld Lang Syne" with George and his friends;
• Supply several boxes of tissues.

Above all, remember that no person is a failure who gives (or attends) an *It's a Wonderful Life* Party.

Huckleberry's Pie

This classic pie was created to honor two characters in *It's a Wonderful Life*: Clarence, who was so anxious to read Mark Twain's "new book," *The Adventures of Huckleberry Finn*, and Annie, the Bailey family maid, who prepared the pies for the dance at which George Bailey and Mary Hatch fell in love.

Preparation time: 10 minutes
Baking time: 45 to 50 minutes

⅓ cup sugar
⅓ cup flour
½ tsp cinnamon
4 cups fresh berries
1 tb butter
9-inch pie crust

1 Preheat oven to 425°.
2 Stir together sugar, flour, cinnamon, and berries. Pour into pie crust. Dot with butter.
3 Bake for 45 to 50 minutes. Let cool and serve.
Yield: 8 slices

Clarence's Flaming Rum Punch

To paraphrase Nick the bartender, this is a hard drink for Spuds who want to get drunk fast. It really packs a wallop, so unless you want to miss the end of the movie, sip it slowly and in moderation. This punch is guaranteed to give your joint atmosphere.

Preparation time: 12 minutes

1 qt cranberry juice cocktail
½ cup sugar
6 strips lemon rind
2 cinnamon sticks
5 whole cloves
1 cup 151-proof rum

1 In a saucepan, heat all ingredients except rum. Let simmer for 10 minutes but do not boil.

2 Strain mixture and discard spices. Add rum.

3 Carefully flame with a long match.

4 Serve immediately in a tall footed glass or Irish coffee mug.

Yield: 4 servings

Guardian Angel Cookies

Mary Bailey might have left these airy coconut delights under the tree for Santa and Clarence. They're also easy to make for Couch Potato parents who are busy having children and running the USO.

Preparation time: 30 minutes
Baking time: 60 minutes

2 egg whites, room temperature
⅛ tsp cream of tartar
¾ cup confectioners' sugar
¼ cup shredded coconut
¼ tsp almond extract

1 Preheat oven to 250°.

2 In a small mixing bowl, beat egg whites and cream of tartar with a mixer on high speed until soft peaks form.

3 Gradually add sugar and continue to beat on high speed until sugar is dissolved.

4 With a rubber spatula, fold in coconut and almond extract.

5 Drop mixture by rounded teaspoonfuls onto lightly greased cookie sheet. Leave a 1-inch space between cookies. Bake for 1 hour or until dry.

6 Cool on wire rack.

Yield: 2 dozen cookies

THE COCOPUFS
(COUNCIL OF COUCH POTATOES UNITED FOR FOOD SAFETY)
REPORT

Eating while watching TV can be fraught with hazards. Sometimes it seems that the only safe thing to do is to stay in bed and eat lettuce. However, Couch Potatoes do not live by lettuce alone. They need and want to snack. For this reason the Council of Couch Potatoes United for Food Safety (COCOPUFS) was formed to advocate safe Couch Potato eating practices.

Once COCOPUFS was established, there developed a nationwide demand for research to determine the causes of food hazards and to provide written guidelines for personal food safety. The COCOPUFS Report is the fruit of our groundbreaking research. It is the first ongoing analysis of popular snack foods designed to rate eaters' safety factors during the act of consumption.

To make The COCOPUFS Report as useful as possible for the food consumer, it has very specific objectives. It rates food safety only *during the act of eating* . . . the time at which most accidents occur. Therefore, questions of taste do not fall within the purview of this report.

Given the confines of the space allotted in this book, we cannot publish the results of our entire survey. This list represents, however, the 25 foods that the Council has determined to be most representative of snack foods available to the general public, and which happen to be the board of directors' favorites.

The COCOPUFS Report

NAME OF PRODUCT*	EASE OF CONTAINER OPENING	MOUTH HAZARDS	INGESTION QUOTIENT	ENTROPY POTENTIAL	TOTAL	COMMENTS
HAAGEN-DAZS SWISS VANILLA ALMOND ICE CREAM	8	5	6	3.5	22.5	Must wait for ice cream to thaw. Not for the very hungry or impatient.
CHEERIOS	7	9	7.5	3	26.5	Easy to drop those small O's.
CHEEZ DOODLES (Puffed)	2	7	6	6.5	21.5	Neighbor in danger from jutting elbows during opening.
CHEX PARTY MIX	3.5	1.5	4	4	13	Different shapes confuse the mouth.
CHIPS AHOY CHOCOLATE CHIP COOKIES	9	7	7.5	8	31.5	Can't be eaten without milk.
COMBOS (Pretzel and cheese)	6	8	4	4.5	22.5	Neat because they are bite-sized.
DEVIL DOGS	3.5	7.5	4	4	19	Best eaten wearing dark clothes.
DORITOS (Original flavor)	8	3	4.5	6	21.5	Hazardous to mouth if eaten whole.
FRITOS (Regular size)	4.5	8	6	4	22.5	Fall easily between cushions.
HOSTESS TWINKIES	3.5	4	8	5.5	21	Can eat only three at one sitting.
JELL-O CHOCOLATE PUDDING POPS	4	7.5	4	3.5	19	Could bite into stick.
M&Ms (Peanut)	9	7	6	2	24	Great roll-under-the-couch problem.
MISTER SALTY VERI-THIN PRETZEL STICKS	6	8	6	4.5	24.5	Difficult to fit large amounts into mouth at one time.

*We have listed the name as it appears on the package.

NAME OF PRODUCT	EASE OF CONTAINER OPENING	MOUTH HAZARDS	INGESTION QUOTIENT	ENTROPY POTENTIAL	TOTAL	COMMENTS
QUAKER S'MORES BARS	4.5	7.5	2.5	6	20.5	Their stickiness lowers their entropy potential.
NILLA WAFERS	5	8.5	9	6	28.5	Good to the last crumb.
OREOS	4	4.5	8	4	20.5	Lends to creative eating techniques, but can cause Oreo Tongue.
PEPPERIDGE FARM'S MILANO COOKIES	6	5.5	8	6	25.5	Entire bag can be eaten by one person during three-hour movie.
PLANTER'S DRY ROASTED MIXED NUTS (Jar)	5	4	6	7.5	22.5	Hard to get what you want out of the narrow jar.
PLANTER'S HONEY ROASTED PEANUTS (Can)	6	8	9	7.5	30.5	Salt and sugar titillate entire tongue.
QUAKER RICE CAKES	7	8	5	6	26	Can't eat whole. Need something spread on it.
RITZ BITS CRACKERS	6	6	8	6	26	Cute and can substitute for missing checker pieces.
SARA LEE'S BUTTER POUND CAKE	7.5	9	9.5	8.5	34.5	Excellent stealth potential.
SLIM JIMS	5	8	5	7	25	A pleasant diversion from sugar, but requires good teeth.
TRISCUITS	5	6	7	8	26	Must bite with the grain to avoid crumbs.
WISE COTTAGE FRIES POTATO CHIPS	5	5	8	5	23	Hazardous to eat in winter; salt burns chapped lips.

This report was compiled purely for humorous purposes and is not meant to be taken as serious scientific data. It reflects only the authors' opinions.

How The COCOPUFS Report Was Compiled

The COCOPUFS Report ranks 25 nationally known snack foods for the following four factors:
- Ease of Container Opening (ECO)
- Mouth Hazards (MH)
- Ingestion Quotient (IQ)
- Entropy Potential (EP)

Guidelines

Ease of Container Opening (ECO)
10   Very easy to open
1   Almost impossible to open without losing some of contents

Mouth Hazards (MH)
10   Glides down throat effortlessly
1   Causes severe lacerations or choking on contact

Ingestion Quotient (IQ)
10   Can be ingested without fear
1   Must be eaten with Alka-Seltzer at hand

Entropy Potential (EP)
(i.e., crumbs, spotting, general spills made during eating)
10   Leaves no trace of its passing on the environment (packaging waste excluded)
1   Cannot be eaten without risk of leaving its mark on the immediate surroundings
(See chart on pages 122-123 for detailed findings.)

Sample Ranking

Rankings run from 1 to 10, with 0.5 increments allowed. For example, an imaginary potato chip-like product called "Potato Fluffies" may be rated as follows:

7.0	Ease of container opening
5.5	Mouth hazards
1.5	Ingestion quotient
2.0	Entropy potential
15.0	Total

In general, a high rating reflects a personally and environmentally safe snack food.

Conclusions

Based on the findings of 14 randomly selected snack-food eaters from the New York metropolitan area, the Sara Lee All-Butter Pound Cake is the safest snack food for Couch Potatoes. It was judged as causing the fewest Mouth Hazards (MH) and being the quietest food. The Chex Party Mix had the highest MH potential, due to its combination of shapes, which confused testers' mouths. Doritos were found to poke the mouth when researchers tried to ingest them whole.

Sara Lee Pound Cake also ranked highest in its Ingestion Quotient (IQ), receiving a 9.5, a nearly perfect (or limitless in edibility) score. Twinkies, Nilla Wafers, Milanos, and Planter's Honey Roasted Peanuts also were judged to be edible in extremely large quantities.

M&Ms and Cheerios received mixed scores. They were given good readings for Ease of Container Opening (ECO), MH, and IQ, but poor scores for their Entropy Potential (EP), which was judged to be high due to their roll-under-the-couch factor.

Chips Ahoy and M&Ms demonstrated the simplest ECO, with nonthreatening pull-apart bags. Cheez Doodles received the lowest ECO rating and its tightly glued bag was judged to be the most hazardous to open in social settings. Twinkies and Devil Dogs were also judged difficult to open because their outside boxes confused our researchers, as did their individual wrappings.

Safety Recommendations for Snack Food Eaters

1 Open all exterior containers before programming begins, including your evening's portions of individually wrapped items.

2 To reduce EP (due to a snack's ability to roll across the room), eat M&Ms and other round snack items individually, if possible.

3 Do not eat large, pointy snack foods whole.

4 It is difficult to make recommendations on IQ, as only each snacker knows his own stomach.

INDEX

About the Authors

Mary Beth Jung is a freelance food journalist, author of *The One Burner Cookbook,* and president of her own public relations firm in Milwaukee. Her favorite programs are "thirtysomething" and "Wall Street Week."

Melinda Corey is an editor and writer who lives in Brooklyn. Her credits include *The Thanksgiving Book.* Her favorite programs are "Moonlighting" and "The Honeymooners."

Jackie Ogburn is a Southerner who works as an editor in New York City. Her favorite programs are "L.A. Law" and World Wrestling Federation bouts.